PASSAGE MEDITATION

A dream is real so long as it lasts. When we awake, we do not pass from unreality to reality; we pass from a lower state of reality to a higher one. Is it not possible that there is a state of awareness higher still, compared with which the limited satisfactions of everyday life are no more lasting than a dream?

EKNATH EASWARAN

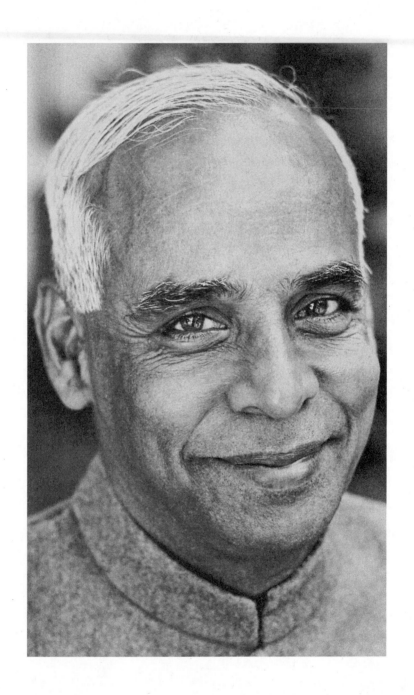

Passage Meditation
A Complete Spiritual Practice

EKNATH EASWARAN

NILGIRI PRESS

First published 1978 as *Meditation: Commonsense Directions for an Uncommon Life*

Fourth edition. First printing September 2016

10 9 8 7 6 5 4

ISBN: 978-1-58638-116-5
eISBN: 978-1-58638-117-2
Audiobook ISBN: 978-1-58638-748-8

New material for this edition comes from the Center's archive of
Eknath Easwaran's teachings.
Library of Congress Control Number: 2016940667

Publisher's Cataloging-In-Publication Data
(Prepared by The Donohue Group, Inc.)

Names: Eknath, Easwaran, 1910-1999.
Title: Passage meditation : a complete spiritual practice : train your mind and find a
life that fulfills / Eknath Easwaran.
Other Titles: Meditation. 1978.
Description: Fourth edition. | Tomales, California : Nilgiri Press, [2016] |
First published in 1978 as: Meditation: commonsense directions for an uncommon
life. | Includes bibliographical references.
Identifiers: LCCN 2016940667 | ISBN 978-1-58638-116-5 | ISBN 978-1-58638-117-2
(ebook) | ISBN 978-1-58638-748-8 (audiobook)
Subjects: LCSH: Meditation. | Meditations.

Classification: LCC BL627 .E17 2016 | DDC 204/.35--dc23

Nilgiri Press is the publishing division of the Blue Mountain Center of Meditation, a
nonprofit organization founded by Eknath Easwaran in 1961.

The Blue Mountain Center of Meditation
www.bmcm.org | info@bmcm.org
Box 256, Tomales, California 94971
Telephone: +1 707 878 2369 Toll-free: 800 475 2369

Printed on FSC® paper

MIX
Paper from
responsible sources
FSC® C103567

Table of Contents

Discovering Meditation

THIS IS THE book I wanted when I began to meditate – direct, simple, practical, and based completely on personal experience. It presents the program I developed for myself in the midst of a very active life on a university campus in India, independent of any established tradition, and first taught systematically at the University of California, Berkeley, in 1968 – probably the first course on meditation ever offered for credit at a major American university.

The method has come to be known as passage meditation because it involves slow, sustained attention on the words of inspired passages chosen from the wisdom literature of the world – scriptures and mystics of all times and cultures. These passages do not belong to any creed or dogma. They are distilled from the experience of men and women who have sought, and discovered, a reality higher and deeper than the world of sense experience. All I have contributed to this legacy is a systematic program for drawing this deep wisdom of the heart into daily life.

Like the passages themselves, the principles and practices this book presents are timeless. But times differ, and our age cries out for universality. Passage meditation can be followed equally well in any religion or in none. It belongs to no movement, asks for no change of beliefs; it simply allows you to take the ideals you respond to and gradually, gracefully, make them part of your life.

I said I developed this program, yet it would be more accurate to say I discovered it. Like a buried treasure, it lay there waiting to be found when I needed it.

At that time, I can honestly say, meditation was the farthest thing from my mind. My days were full with a job I loved, teaching English literature on a beautiful college campus in central India. I had begun to make a reputation as a writer; I had friends with whom to enjoy music, theater, tennis, and the quiet pleasures of good company; everything I wanted was flowing into my hands. It was a very satisfying situation, and if I had had time to think about it, I would have assured you I was happy.

Instead, I was surprised to find myself feeling empty inside. Something deep could not be satisfied. Old, old questions began to come unbidden as I lay awake at night: *Why am I here? What is life for? What happens when I die?*

Nothing in my education had prepared me for such questions. Nothing I read could answer them for me. Only when I discovered meditation did I find the higher vantage I needed to see life whole — and that discovery opened the door to a way of life so much more fulfilling that my days before seem like a dream.

As so often happens, it was death that precipitated the crisis. In a few short months, one after the other, I lost people passionately dear to me: Mahatma Gandhi, who had been my beacon since college; my beloved grandmother, my spiritual teacher; then a friend almost exactly my age. Systematically, every support I leaned on had been dashed away. With my world upside down, I came home from a walk one day and found that one of my dogs, who doted on me, had been run over by a passing truck. It was as if she stood for all of us: for Gandhi and Granny and everyone else who had died; for all of us still living, for whom death was simply biding time.

Instinctively, like so many before me, I turned to traditional wisdom. I was not at all religious, but at an early age I had fallen in love with India's best-known scripture, the Bhagavad Gita, simply because of its poetry. I knew most of the verses by heart; nothing could be more natural than to turn to them in a time of crisis. I remember sitting down with eyes closed and letting the words roll through my consciousness:

> Never was the Self born; never shall it
> Cease to be. Without beginning or end,
> Free from birth, free from death, and free from time,
> How can the Self die when the body dies?

The words must have taken me in, because when I opened my eyes at last it had grown dark. Time had been suspended, and the burden of sorrow was gone. I felt as if I had returned from another world – an inner realm beyond time and space where somehow I was at home.

Over the next few weeks I revisited those verses, and many others, in the same way, seated in silence in the early morning, drawn by the way the words nourished my consciousness and anchored my life. Gradually it dawned on me that there was ancient tradition behind what I was doing. I was *meditating* – becoming absorbed in the words of the Gita just as I had seen Mahatma Gandhi doing years before. India had refined this to a science thousands of years ago, but I had known nothing of it. I had been looking everywhere for a treasure hidden at home.

I have to admit the realization frightened me. I had no intention of entering on what I thought must be an otherworldly path, and no desire whatever to follow a way of life that meant leaving the world behind. I was a modern man with family and friends, and I loved my students and my work. I was not about to leave everything and retire to a Himalayan cave.

In addition, I felt lost in this new world within. My Western education had left me without roots. It would be many years before I understood that this helped make my experience accessible to millions of others who, like me, felt adrift in a world that denies the reality of anything beyond the senses.

Always a reader, I turned to books to understand the adventure I had embarked on. Instead of philosophy and psychology, however, I turned to the world's mystics—people like Mahatma Gandhi and Teresa of Avila who had undertaken this journey and written not from theory or speculation, but from personal experience.

I read widely, drawing no distinction between East and West; I cared only whether the testimonies were authentic. I discovered the Upanishads, and through them India's tremendous spiritual heritage. Patanjali's classic text on meditation helped greatly in providing the framework my intellectual training required. I read the Catholic mystics, the Buddhist scriptures, the passionate poetry of the Sufis. I discovered that religion has nothing to do with dogma, theology, or anything else that divides. Religion is *realization*: making the truths of the world's great scriptures a reality in daily life.

Aldous Huxley's *The Perennial Philosophy,* with its selection of quotations from mystics of all religions, provided my first glimpse that the voyage I had embarked on was not unique but universal. Throughout history, I discovered, men and women of all faiths and backgrounds had stumbled onto a hidden path that led to the same destination, the heartland of the spirit within. The paths varied according to creed and culture, but the journey was the same. "The mystics must come from the same country," Saint-Martin wrote, "for they all speak the same language."

In this way I discovered other voices, in beautiful passages for meditation from every major spiritual tradition. Often it was monastics who spoke, but I found a few who, like me, had chosen not to withdraw into monasteries but to seek a higher reality right in the midst of everyday affairs. I had stumbled upon a way to bring the ancient art of meditation out of the cloister into daily life.

In meditation I found a deep connection between the wisdom in those passages and the way I conducted myself throughout the day. It was a thrilling discovery. Certain skills, such as slowing down and focusing on one thing at a time, deepened my concentration during meditation, and in turn that brought depth to whatever I did during the rest of the day. The passages were lifelines, guiding me to the source of wisdom deep within and then guiding me back into daily life.

All this time I was continuing a very full life at the university, with a heavy load of classes accompanied by administrative duties and a good deal of time given over to students in the evening. Making time for meditation was a continuing challenge, but the benefits were so great that I made it my first priority. As systematically as a professional athlete, I worked on my daily life, building it around the regular daily practice of meditation.

Years passed like this. Both within and without, my life became even busier, richer, more challenging as my meditation deepened.

In 1959, I had the opportunity to go to the United States as a Fulbright scholar, part of an exchange program aimed at international understanding. That proved to be the beginning of a new career, a shift from education for degrees to education for living. In the US, I lectured widely on the spiritual heritage of India. Often, people would come up after the talks to ask questions, and some were eager to learn how to meditate. I have always enjoyed teaching; sharing what I love comes naturally. I studied everything I had learned from my own practice and worked on a way to present it simply, practically, and systematically. In this way I distilled from those years of effort an eight-point program for daily living based on passage meditation.

This method has two characteristics. The first is the training of attention, which gradually draws together the scattered threads of what one thinks, feels, says, and does. In this process conflicts resolve, gradually bringing about the complete integration of personality.

The second aspect of passage meditation derives from the passages themselves — or, rather, from the power that comes from sustained concentration when the words open their doors and release their meaning. I can find no better way to put it. The experience is not intellectual, and I am not talking about dictionary definitions; the truths the passages express simply become part of one's life, assimilated into character and consciousness just as the nutrients in food become part of the body. In the simplest possible language, this is the secret of meditation: we become what we meditate on.

Here are the eight points of this program:

1. Meditation on a Passage
2. Repetition of a Mantram
3. Slowing Down
4. One-Pointed Attention
5. Training the Senses
6. Putting Others First
7. Spiritual Fellowship
8. Spiritual Reading

It is essential that all eight of these be practiced daily. Though they may at first seem unrelated, they are closely linked. Quieting your mind in morning meditation, for instance, will help your efforts to slow down at work, and slowing down at work will, in turn, improve your meditation. But suppose you try to follow only part of this program. Hurry at work and your mind will race during meditation; skip meditation and you will find it difficult to be both slow and concentrated. In other words, some of the steps generate spiritual power while others put it to wise use during the day. Unless you practice all of them, you cannot progress safely and far.

I am still surprised to see the immense potential of this simple program. Without intending it, I had found a path that anyone can follow — a path with all the richness and depth of traditional wisdom, regardless of one's culture or belief, together with a practical method for bringing that wisdom into daily life. By the time I was asked to teach meditation on the Berkeley campus, I had worked out a systematic presentation that, like a good professor, I could sketch on the board and fill out week by week in a semester of talks.

Out of those classes, tested further over the next ten years, came this book.

In India, meditation is called "the end of sorrow" and "mastery of the art of living." It is my deepest prayer that through this book you will find these promises fulfilled in your own life.

PASSAGE MEDITATION

Part I. Passage Meditation: An Eight-Point Program

Meditation on a Passage

I AM GOING to suppose that your purpose in picking up this book is to learn to meditate; so I will begin straight away with some instructions.

I recommend beginning with the Prayer of Saint Francis of Assisi. If you already know another passage, such as the Twenty-third Psalm, it will do nicely until you have learned this prayer. But over many years of teaching meditation, I have found that Saint Francis's words have an almost universal appeal. Through them pulses the spiritual wisdom this gentle friar drew upon when he undertook the most awesome task a human being is capable of: the total transformation of character, conduct, and consciousness. The prayer goes like this:

> Lord, make me an instrument of thy peace.
> Where there is hatred, let me sow love;
> Where there is injury, pardon;
> Where there is doubt, faith;
> Where there is despair, hope;
> Where there is darkness, light;
> Where there is sadness, joy.

O divine Master, grant that I may not so much seek
To be consoled as to console,
To be understood as to understand,
To be loved as to love;
For it is in giving that we receive;
It is in pardoning that we are pardoned;
It is in dying to self that we are born to eternal life.

I hope you will understand that the word "Lord" here does not refer to a white-bearded gentleman ruling from a throne somewhere between Neptune and Pluto. When I use words like "Lord" or "God," I mean the very ground of existence, the most profound thing we can conceive of. This supreme reality is not something outside us, something separate from us. It is within, at the core of our being — our real nature, nearer to us than our bodies, dearer to us than our lives.

If you prefer a passage from another tradition, here are some other popular choices I recommend:

LAO TZU: THE BEST

The best, like water,
Benefit all and do not compete.
They dwell in lowly spots that everyone else scorns.
Putting others before themselves,
They find themselves in the foremost place
And come very near to the Tao.
In their dwelling, they love the earth;
In their heart, they love what is deep;
In personal relationships, they love kindness;

In their words, they love truth.
In the world, they love peace.
In personal affairs, they love what is right.
In action, they love choosing the right time.
It is because they do not compete with others
That they are beyond the reproach of the world.

A SONG OF DAVID: PSALM 23

The Lord is my shepherd; I shall not want.
He maketh me to lie down in green pastures;
He leadeth me beside the still waters.
He restoreth my soul; He guideth me
in straight paths for His name's sake.
Yea, though I walk through the valley
of the shadow of death, I will fear no evil,
for Thou art with me;
Thy rod and Thy staff, they comfort me.
Thou preparest a table before me in the presence
of mine enemies; Thou hast anointed my head
with oil; my cup runneth over.
Surely goodness and mercy shall follow me
all the days of my life; and I shall dwell
in the house of the Lord forever.

RIG VEDA: UNITED IN HEART

May we be united in heart.
May we be united in speech.
May we be united in mind.

May we perform our duties
As did the wise of old.

May we be united in our prayer.
May we be united in our goal.
May we be united in our resolve.
May we be united in our understanding.
May we be united in our offering.
May we be united in our feelings.
May we be united in our hearts.
May we be united in our thoughts.
May there be perfect unity amongst us.

Having memorized the passage, be seated and softly close your eyes. We defeat the purpose of meditation if we look about, admiring the bird on the sill or watching people come and go. The eyes, ears, and other senses are rather like appliances with their cords plugged into the mind. During meditation, we try to pull out the plugs so we can concentrate more fully on the words of the passage. To disconnect the senses — to leave the world of sound behind, for instance — is difficult. We may even believe that it is not possible, that everything has been permanently installed. But the mystics testify that these cords can be disconnected and that when we do this, we experience a serenity beyond words.

So shut your eyes — without getting tense about it. Since the body should be relaxed, not strained, there is no need to be effortful. The best teacher for eye-closing I have seen is a baby... tired lids gently sliding down on tired eyes.

PACE

Once you have memorized a passage, you are ready to go through it word by word, as slowly as you can. Why slowly? I think it is Meher Baba, a modern mystic of India, who explained:

A mind that is fast is sick.
A mind that is slow is sound.
A mind that is still is divine.

Think of a car tearing along at ninety miles per hour. The driver may feel exuberant, powerful, but a number of things can suddenly cause him to lose control. When he is moving at thirty miles per hour, his car handles easily; even if somebody else makes a dangerous maneuver, he can probably turn and avoid a collision. So too with the mind. When its desperate whirrings slow down, intentionality and good judgment appear, then love, and finally what the Bible calls "the peace that passes understanding." Let the words, therefore, proceed slowly. You can cluster the small helper words with a word of substance, like this:

Lord … make … me … an instrument … of thy … peace.

The space between words is a matter for each person to work out individually. They should be comfortably spaced with a little elbowroom between. If the words come too close together, you will not be slowing down the mind:

Lord.make.me.

If the words stand too far apart, they will not be working together:

Lord … … make

Here "make" has put in its contribution, but "me" simply won't get on with it. Before long some other word or image or idea rushes in to fill the vacuum, and the passage has been lost.

With some experimentation, you will find your own best pace. I remember that when I learned to drive many years ago, my instructor kept trying patiently to teach me to use the clutch. I was not a terribly apt pupil. After a number of chugging stops and dying engines, I asked him how I was ever going to master those pedals. He said, "You get a feeling for it." That is the way with the words too: you will know intuitively when not enough space lies between them and when there is too much.

Concentrate on one word at a time, and let the words slip one after another into your consciousness like pearls falling into a clear pond. Let them all drop inwards one at a time. Of course, we learn this skill gradually. For some time we drop a word and it floats on the surface, bumped around by distractions, irrelevant imagery, fantasies, worries, regrets, and negative emotions. At least we see just how far we are from being able to give the mind a simple order that it will carry out.

Later on, after assiduous practice, the words will fall inward; you will see them going in and hitting the very bottom. This takes time, though. Don't expect it to happen next week. Nothing really worth having comes quickly and easily; if it did, I doubt that we would ever grow.

As you attend to each word dropping singly, significantly, into your consciousness, you will realize that there is no discrepancy between sound and meaning. When you concentrate on the sound of each word, you will also be concentrating on the meaning of the passage. Sound and sense are one.

Trying to visualize the words—imagining them in your mind's eye, or even typing them mentally as some people want to do—may help a little at the outset, but later on it will become an obstacle. We are working to shut down the senses temporarily, and visualization only binds us to the sensory level of consciousness.

Your body may even try to get into the act. I recall a lady who not only typed her passage mentally but danced her fingers quite unknowingly along an imaginary keyboard too. Another friend used to sway back and forth in meditation as if she were singing in a choir. So check yourself occasionally to see that you are not developing any superfluous body movements.

DISTRACTIONS

As you go through the passage, do not follow any association of ideas. Just keep to the words. Despite your best efforts, you will find this extremely difficult. You will begin to realize what an accomplished trickster the mind is, to what lengths it will go to evade your sovereignty.

Let us say you reach the end of the first line: "...an instrument...of thy...peace." So far your mind has been fully on the passage and has not wandered at all. Excellent! But at the word *peace* the mind asks, "Who is the Prince of Peace?"

Well, it has raised a very spiritual question, and you say, "Jesus Christ."

"Do you know where the Prince of Peace was born?" the mind returns quickly.

"Yes, Bethlehem."

"Have you heard about Bethlehem Steel?"

And you're off. "Oh, yes. In fact, my father had shares in it."

"Oh, yeah," says the mind. "What happened?"

Now, you are supposed to be meditating on the words of Saint Francis, but you continue with this absurd dialogue. This is the sort of thing you really have to be on the lookout for. Don't let your mind wander from the words of the inspirational passage. If you want to ruminate on the stock exchange, get a copy of the *Wall Street Journal* and study it later. Under no circumstances should you try to answer questions or recall things during meditation. That is exactly what the mind wants; it tries to escape and become enmeshed in something – anything – else. The only strategy is to keep your concentration on the passage as much and as long as you can. It will be very difficult at times.

Suppose that the mind does get completely away from you. What should you do? In football, as you know, certain penalties are part of the game, and in meditation too a penalty should be applied when the mind becomes unruly. Be fair, and state the rules the first day. In plain language say, "I'm sorry, but if you run away from the passage, you will have to go back to the beginning and start again."

The mind will pale on hearing that, and for a while it will be hesitant to leave. It may stand up, look around, glance at you, perhaps meander over near the door. But you should not apply the penalty yet – the door is still closed; the mind has not gone out. As long as you are on the passage and have not forgotten about it completely, even if there is some division of attention, don't apply the penalty; just concentrate harder.

But when the door has opened, when the mind has jumped in its sports car and sped away, when you find yourself in a dress shop or a bookstore or at the beach, act promptly. Go up and tap the mind gently on the shoulder. It will probably cringe and say, "You're furious with me, aren't you?"

Still another trick, the rascal! It actually wants you to become angry and start scolding, because then it won't have to return to the passage. Don't get impatient or rattled. Say with perfect courtesy, "This is a poor time to go browsing for a best-seller. Won't you kindly rejoin me in the room where we're meditating on the Prayer of Saint Francis?" And gently take the mind back to the first line: "Lord, make me ..." If the escape occurred during the second stanza, start at the beginning of that stanza. This is hard work, and the mind will get the point.

When we take our dog Muka for a walk along a country road, he sometimes sees a cow and dashes ahead to upset her. To prevent this, we call him back. Further on he sees another cow and starts to trot forward ever so slightly, hoping we won't notice. Again, someone has to call out, "Muka!" He circles back. But after a little while his attention gets caught again, and he edges in front. This goes on ceaselessly.

Bringing the mind back when it strays is like that. But though you may have to do it many times, this is not a pointless activity, not a wasted effort. Saint Francis of Sales explains, "Even if you did nothing during the whole of your hour but bring your mind back and place it again in our Lord's presence, though it went away every time you brought it back, your hour would be very well employed."

Then, too – unlike Muka – your mind will learn. Today you may have to bring it back fifteen times, perhaps thirty. But in three years, you may bring it back only a few times; in six years, perhaps twice; in ten years, not at all.

Occasionally the mind may try the old recorder ruse. You are repeating correctly, "It is in giving that we receive," when a garbled version comes on: "It is in grabbing that we receive." If this happens, don't become agitated and try forcefully to turn off this unwelcome sound track. You may believe that you can do this with some effort, but actually you will only amplify the distracting voice. By dwelling on it, by struggling against it, you simply make it more powerful. The best course is to attend more to the true words of the prayer. The more attention you give them, the less you will be giving to the garbled version. When your attention rests completely on the passage, there can be no attention on anything else.

So when distractions come, just ignore them. When, for instance, you are acutely aware of noises around you while meditating, concentrate harder on the words of the passage. For a while you may still hear the cars passing by, but the day will come when you hear them no longer. When I first moved to Berkeley, I lived in an ancient apartment house on a busy street. My friends said I would never be able to meditate there – "Nothing but ambulances, helicopters, and rock bands," they told me. I sat down for meditation at twilight, and for five minutes I heard it all. After that, I might just as well have been in a remote corner of the Gobi Desert.

THE PASSAGE

You may wonder why I recommend an inspirational passage for meditation. First, it is training in concentration. Most of our mental powers are so widely dispersed that they are relatively ineffective. When I was a boy, I used to hold a lens over paper until the sun's rays gathered to an intense focus and set the paper aflame. In meditation, we gradually focus the mind so that when we meet a difficulty, we can cut right through the nonessentials.

Second, we begin to resemble and actually become whatever we give our attention to. People who think and dream about money have minds pervaded by dimes and dollars, shares and properties, profit and loss. Everything they see, everything they do, is colored by this concern. Similarly with those who dwell on power, revenge, pleasure, or fame. For this reason the Buddha opened his Dhammapada with the magnificent line, "All that we are is the result of what we have thought." And today, despite our technology and science, people are most insecure because they persist in thinking about and going after things that have no capacity to give them security.

An inspirational passage turns our thoughts to what is permanent, to those things that put a final end to insecurity. In meditation, the passage becomes imprinted on our consciousness. As we drive it deeper and deeper, the words come to life within us, transforming all our thoughts, feelings, words, and deeds.

For this reason, please don't try to improve upon the words of the prayer or change them in any way. Just as they stand, they embody the spiritual wisdom of Saint Francis. When Ali Baba wanted to enter the cave of the forty thieves, he had to have the right password. He could yell out, "Open, brown rice" or "Open, shredded wheat" forever, but nothing was going to happen until he said, "Open, sesame." Meditate on Saint Francis's own words, and you will find that you begin to resonate with the spirit of self-forgetfulness and love that the words contain.

Using the same passage over and over is fine at the outset, but in time, the words may seem stale. You may find yourself repeating them mechanically, without sensitivity to their meaning. I suggest you memorize new pieces from the traditions of Buddhism, Christianity, Judaism, Hinduism, and Islam so you will have a varied repertoire. As you commit a new passage to memory, it is good to spend some time reflecting on the meaning of the words and their practical application to your life. But please don't do this while you are actually meditating.

In selecting a passage, be sure it really inspires. Don't let yourself be carried away by literary beauty or novelty. Wordsworth and Shelley may have been splendid poets, but for passages on which to remake your life, I suggest you draw only on the scriptures and the great mystics of the world. And avoid choosing passages that are negative, that take a harsh and deprecatory view of the body, of our past mistakes, or of life in the world. We want to draw forth our positive side, our higher Self, and the passages should move you to become steadfast, compassionate, and wise.

Keeping a notebook of pieces to memorize may help. Later on, after you have learned to concentrate well and need a greater challenge, try a longer work. I find the Katha Upanishad, for instance, perfect for meditation. It is lengthy and complex; you have to be alert to use it. When it goes smoothly, you will feel you are traveling down one lane of a six-lane highway, such an expert driver that you hardly have to move a hand.

Once I went with an old friend to a meeting in the hills. The road twisted continuously, and his driving impressed me. On hairpin turns in India I have seen drivers lunge and clasp the wheel tightly, their faces grimly set. But my friend took each curve with an easy spin of the wheel, letting it swing back on its own.

"That's amazing," I said. "How in the world did you ever manage to learn that?"

He answered tersely, "Machines obey me."

This is a good analogy with the mind that is disciplined in meditation. When we are fully concentrated on the passage, the mind obeys us. It will make the exact turn necessary. We know the road, the curves, the precipices, and where we felt intimidated before, now there is the satisfaction of mastery.

TIME

The best time for meditation is early in the morning. In a tropical country like India, "early" has to be very early — sometimes three o'clock in traditional ashrams. But in a milder climate, I would say between five and six is a reasonable hour to begin, depending on your schedule. Starting the day early enables you to take a short walk or do some exercises, meditate, and have a leisurely breakfast with your family or friends. It sets a relaxing mood for the rest of the day.

The dawn brings freshness, renewal. Birds and other creatures know this; we, "the crown of creation," do not seem to. I have met a few students who were very late risers indeed. I teased one of them by saying, "Have you ever seen a sunrise?" He smiled sheepishly. "Never. But a friend of mine once did."

At first, true, there may be conflict about leaving your bed as the first rays of the sun peep in, especially when the weather is chilly. I have a simple suggestion for young people: give one mighty leap, right out of bed! Don't think — just act. To become more alert, you might try a headstand or shoulder stand, or a few exercises. Older people, of course, can creep out of bed more slowly. But they too should be up as early as reasonable, at least by six o'clock.

I have found a great aid to rising early: settling into bed early. I am not saying sundown or eight o'clock, but ten seems to me a reasonable and healthful time to go to bed — very much the middle path, which avoids extremes.

Whenever I forgot to perform an errand for my grandmother, she would ask, "Have you ever forgotten your breakfast?" No, I had to confess, I hadn't, nor had anybody else I knew. Strike a bargain with yourself — no meditation, no breakfast — and you won't forget to meditate.

It helps, too, to have your meditation at the same time every morning. It will become a reflex. At five-thirty you will feel a tugging at your sleeve, a reminder to get up and begin your meditation.

For those beginning to meditate, half an hour is the requisite period. Less than that will not be enough; more than that may be hazardous. I want to stress it. Please do not, in a burst of enthusiasm, increase your meditation to an hour or longer, because such a practice exposes you to dangers.

What dangers? Most people do not have much concentration; while they are still learning to meditate, they will remain on the surface level of consciousness. But a few have an inborn capacity to plunge deeply inward. And once you break through the surface level, you are in an uncharted world. It is like a desert, but instead of sand there are latent psychological tendencies, terribly powerful forces. There you stand in that vast desert without a compass. You have tapped forces before you are prepared to handle them, and your daily life can be adversely affected.

So please stick to half an hour in the morning and do not increase the time without the advice of an experienced teacher. I do not encourage those who meditate with me to increase the period of meditation until I have inquired into their patterns of daily living and made sure that they practice the other seven steps in this program. If you want to meditate more, have half an hour at night before going to bed.

Someone once approached me with a furrowed brow. "I went beyond my half hour this morning — have I damaged my nervous system?"

"How much longer did you go?" I asked.

"Five minutes."

Well, nothing is going to happen if you meditate five or six minutes more. But don't meditate five minutes less.

Actually, it is best not to be concerned about time during meditation itself. Whenever you are aware of time, a distracting element has entered. After twelve minutes some people think, "Only eighteen minutes more." Or they look at their watches every few minutes. Once you start meditating, forget about time. There is no need to keep checking the clock; with practice you will be able to time your meditation pretty well.

Of course, having ample time for meditation helps free you from worrying about when to stop. Another good reason for getting up early! In this way you won't have to cut things too closely. Twenty-nine minutes for meditation, fourteen minutes for breakfast, eight minutes to complete a project before you leave — you know the story. Give yourself plenty of time for all the essential activities.

PLACE

It is helpful if you can set aside a room in your home just for meditation and nothing else, a room that will begin to have strong spiritual associations for you. Hearing that, people sometimes object, "A separate room for meditation? I only have one room... where will I sleep? Where will I keep my clothes?" Well, if you cannot have an entire room, reserve at least one corner. But whatever you use, keep it only for meditation. Don't talk about money or possessions or frivolous things there; don't give vent to angry words. Gradually, your room or corner will become holy.

The scriptures say that the place of meditation should be calm, clean, and cool. I would add, well-ventilated – and, if possible, quiet. If there are spiritual figures who appeal to you deeply – Jesus, the Buddha, Saint Teresa, Sri Ramakrishna – have a picture of one or two. But otherwise the place should be very simple, even austere, not cluttered with furniture and other things. Let the graceful economy of the traditional Japanese home be your guide.

I sometimes receive catalogs advertising special paraphernalia required for meditation. I must have a cosmic mandala cushion, sit in a pyramid, and inhale only Astral Vision brand Illumination Incense. In meditation, the only equipment you really need is the will, and you can't buy that through the mail.

It is good to meditate with others. Ideally, the whole family can use the same room and meditate together; it strengthens their relationships. Similarly, even if they don't live in the same house, two or three friends can gather together in one home for morning and evening meditation. You will remember that Jesus said, "Where two or three come together in my name, I am present among them,"

POSTURE

The correct posture for meditation is to sit erect with the spinal column, the nape of the neck, and the head in a straight line: not like a ramrod, rigid and tense, but easily upright. Your hands may be placed any way they feel comfortable. You will find it a very natural position.

If you want to sit in a straight-back chair, use one with arms. Should you become a bit forgetful of your body, you won't tip over in such a chair. Or you can sit cross-legged on a cushion on the floor. You needn't try to assume the classic "full lotus" posture, which most people find quite demanding. Your body should be comfortable – but not so comfortable that you cannot remain alert.

I want to emphasize this matter of posture because it is so easy to become careless. In meditation, people can be quite unaware of what their bodies are doing. Some twist around in the most amazing manner. Once, on the Berkeley campus – where strange events have been known to occur – I opened my eyes and saw someone meditating without a head. For a moment, I was stunned. Then I realized that somehow this fellow had managed to drop his head back over his chair, an advanced acrobatic feat. After meditation he came up to me and said, "I have a problem. I am hung up in time."

"My dear friend," I thought to myself, "you are hung up in space." So without dwelling on it, check yourself occasionally in meditation to see that your head is in place – that you are not twisting around, leaning over, drooping like a question mark, or swaying back and forth. Particularly when your mind wanders away from the passage, or you become drowsy or enter a deeper state of consciousness, verify once in a while that your posture is still correct.

The appropriate dress for meditation has nothing to do with fashion. Simply wear loose-fitting garments, things that keep you from becoming too warm or too cool. Basically, clothes you feel comfortable in will do nicely.

DROWSINESS

You may have noticed how tense you feel when you are agitated, and how relaxing it feels to be absorbed in something. In meditation, of course, we welcome deep concentration. But it does bring with it a difficulty that will be with us for a long time – with relaxation comes the tendency to fall asleep. As concentration improves and the neuromuscular system begins to relax in meditation, a wave of drowsiness may come to you. A beatific look spreads across your face, you begin to nod, and that's it.

Once, after I had been meditating with friends, the fellow sitting next to me confided, "I really had a good meditation tonight!" I wouldn't have called it good, but it was certainly audible. What he actually had was about twenty-five minutes of pure sleep.

So now I have to tell you something unpleasant. As soon as sleep begins oozing through you, just at the moment you are really beginning to feel marvelous, move away from your back support and let the wave of drowsiness pass over your head. Do not give in. At the very first sign of sleepiness, draw yourself up, keep your spinal column quite erect, and give even more attention to the passage. This will not be fun. But if you say, "Oh, I'll enjoy a few more minutes of this delicious drowsiness and then ..." – well, in a few minutes you will not be able to do anything about it.

You may have to resist sleep for a long time. But if you do not resist now, whenever a wave of drowsiness comes, there will be trouble ahead. Later on, when you enter the depths of the unconscious in meditation, you will not be able to remain alert. I have seen people meditating with their heads on their chests, and it is extremely difficult to deal with the problem then. If from the earliest days you can remain awake throughout meditation, you will be able to descend from the surface level right into the unconscious and walk about completely aware.

So whenever you feel sleepy in meditation, or the words seem fuzzy or slip away, draw yourself up. It may be necessary to repeat this over and over again. If you are still unable to dispel the drowsiness, open your eyes and continue with the passage or repeat the mantram for a minute or two, as explained in the next chapter. But don't let your eyes wander, or your mind will wander too. It helps to have a focus for attention that will not distract you from your meditation – perhaps a picture of a great mystic or spiritual teacher whom you find inspiring.

Of course, I am assuming in all this that you have had your legitimate quota of rest the previous night. If you have not, drowsiness in meditation will surely defeat you.

The problem of sleep can be distressing, but it is also reassuring. It means that your nervous system has begun to relax, that the feverish pace of the mind has begun to slow down and that new challenges are presenting themselves to you.

PHYSICAL SENSATIONS

Deepening meditation and the physiological changes that accompany it require a body that works beautifully at all times. We must do what we can to make the body a good ally. We must give it what it needs: adequate sleep every night, wholesome, nourishing food in reasonable quantities, and lots of vigorous movement. Without a balance between physical activity and meditation, for instance, we may become irritable or restless. Exercise – jogging, swimming, climbing, hard work, and so forth for young people, and walking for just about everybody – can help to solve some of the problems that come as you descend in consciousness.

I would like to advise you of some of the little physical annoyances you may meet during meditation. When you sit down, the mind can line up scores of these and say, "Okay, boys, here we go! Now, one at a time!" Then the eerie sensations parade before you: you feel your left foot swelling; you feel a creature inching up and down your spine; you feel some dizziness, nausea, itching, tightness, or salivation.

Broadly speaking, these sensations are nothing more than stratagems of the mind to resist being brought under control. It wants to distract you and will use any trick. The Marquis of Queensberry rules simply do not apply. If you say, "That's not fair," the mind will answer, "What does this curious word *fair* mean?"

Never allow these annoyances to become an excuse for skipping meditation. If you do, the next day will be harder, because the mind has won a round.

When strange sensations trouble you, it is helpful to be sure the meditation room is ventilated, wear loose clothes, and have plenty of exercise during the day.

If you feel too hot, I would suggest that you also avoid stimulants, overheated rooms, and clothes that are too warm, sleep at night with windows open if you can, and drink plenty of liquids.

(I have found fresh fruit juices and buttermilk especially helpful.)

Try not to dwell on these sensations, but give more attention to the words of the passage. When you concentrate more, you will probably find that these distractions disappear. But if your ears are ringing and you start to swat them, they will just ring louder.

If you are meditating with others, then sneezes and coughs (and their cousins – yawns, hiccoughs, sniffles, and snorts) not only tyrannize you but other people too. One sneeze and every-body's meditation may be interrupted for a time. Do what you can to minimize these respiratory outbursts and preserve the quiet.

Similarly, it is a thoughtful act, a spiritual act, to enter and leave the meditation room silently, so you do not disturb others. Turn the door latch gently; tiptoe in and out; place your cushion and lap blanket, if you have one, quietly and mindfully. And use discretion in calling someone out of meditation. Do not do it unless a critical need arises – and if you must interrupt, please don't stride up to them speaking in a loud voice or try to shake them vigor-ously; it can be a real shock to the nervous system. Touching the person with a bird's lightness and waiting a few moments will probably be enough to make him or her aware of your presence.

You may find you need to reposition your arms or legs during meditation because they are going to sleep, or because you feel some fatigue, cramps, or tension there. It is not helpful to be too indulgent, of course, and move at every slight discomfort, but there does come an appropriate time to make some adjustment in position. Here, too, do it as quietly as possible and without altering your upright posture.

If you discover at the end of your period of meditation that your legs have gone to sleep, you can sit for a few minutes and massage them gently instead of trying to rise. In fact, I would say that it is better not to jump right up after meditation at all, especially for beginners, because your legs may have gone to sleep without your being aware of it.

DANGERS IN MEDITATION

Strong emotions may be activated during meditation. Occasionally, for example, someone will be afraid of breaking through the surface level of consciousness to a deeper level. Should this happen to you, open your eyes for a minute or two and repeat the mantram in your mind. Then close your eyes again and resume the passage. If the fear returns, repeat the process. Having a picture of a great mystic nearby may help here too.

Waves of positive emotion can also sweep over a meditator. A few get so moved they weep. Such a purging of pent-up emotion may be very beneficial. But it becomes an obstacle if you dwell on it, get excited about it, run to report it to everybody. A great Catholic mystic warns those who bask in this emotion that they may turn into bees caught in their own honey. When you go on concentrating on the passage even during waves of emotion, your meditation is immeasurably deepened.

Earlier I mentioned the mind's many tricks and distractions, and here I can add one of its cleverest: tempting us with interior stimuli. You may see lights, perhaps brilliant ones, or hear sounds. Some people are fascinated by such things; they become hypnotized by the eruptions of light, by the colors and shapes. They relax their hold on the passage and stay back to watch the show. Exactly what the mind wants! This impresario will stage endless spectacles if you are content to stop and gawk.

We can see the most gorgeous interior fireworks and still be impatient in our daily living. And we can progress far on the spiritual path and never meet any of these things. So whatever you see – lights, lines, colors, shapes, faces, trees – do not stop to give your attention to them, but concentrate more on the words.

Entering deeper consciousness is like descending into a cave. There are bewitching experiences, and there can also be awesome, even disorienting ones. Just as the spelunker uses a rope to thread his way downward, the meditator's lifeline is the passage. No matter what happens in meditation, never loosen your grip on the passage! It will guide you through all situations. If you do lose the words for a second, come back to them immediately.

One last warning: please do not try to connect the passage to a physiological function, such as heartbeat or breathing rhythm. Such a connection may seem helpful initially, but it can cause serious problems later. When you give your full attention to the passage, your breathing cycle slows down naturally and all the functions of the body begin to work in harmony; there is no need to force them into line.

RENEWING OUR COMMITMENT

To make progress in meditation, you must be regular in your practice of it. Some people catch fire at the beginning, but when the novelty wears off in a few days and the hard work sets in, their fires dampen and go out. They cut back, postpone, make excuses, perhaps feel guilty and apologetic. This is precisely where our determination is tested, where we can ask ourselves, "Do I really want to get over my problems? Do I want to claim my birthright of joy, love, and peace of mind? Do I want to discover the meaning of life and of my own life?"

There is only one failure in meditation: the failure to meditate faithfully. A Hindu proverb says, "Miss one morning, and you need seven to make it up." Or as Saint John of the Cross expressed it, "He who interrupts the course of his spiritual exercises and prayer is like a man who allows a bird to escape from his hand; he can hardly catch it again."

Put your meditation first and everything else second; you will find, for one thing, that it enriches everything else. Even if you are on a jet or in a sickbed, don't let that come in the way of your practice. If you are harassed by personal anxieties, it is all the more important to have your meditation; it will release the resources you need to solve the problems at hand.

To make progress in meditation, we have to be not only systematic but sincere too. It won't do to sit and go through the mental motions halfheartedly. We need to renew our enthusiasm and commitment every day and give our best all the time. Success comes to those who keep at it — walking when they cannot run, crawling when they cannot walk, never saying "No, I can't do this," but always "I'll keep trying."

Have you heard the expression "heroes at the beginning"? All enthusiasm for the first few days, but then ... Not long ago I watched the news coverage of the annual Bay to Breakers run, from one side of San Francisco to the other. Some fifteen thousand people showed up to participate ... brand new color-coordinated outfits, top-rated running shoes, digital stopwatches, everything you could want for a serious race. And what enthusiasm at the start! Everyone bouncing along with jaunty, springing steps, grinning at the spectators, scanning the competition for an attractive face…this is the life!

The next morning, though, I read about the aftermath. Fifteen thousand may have started, but thousands never finished. Sure, at the beginning, everything feels fine. But out around Hayes Street – after the downtown traffic, the noise, the fumes – a lot of people begin to think twice. The pavement is hot…and so are those top-rated running shoes. Hills are coming up, and the attractive face that refreshed your eyes has disappeared over the next rise. Up ahead a billboard asks, "Wouldn't a nice cold beer taste *good* right now?" Next thing you know, you're sitting on a stool at Roy's Recovery Room, watching the end of the pack trudge along and thinking, "Next year …"

It helps to know at the outset that you will be running a marathon in this program, not simply jogging once or twice around a track. It is good to be enthusiastic when you sit down for meditation the first morning; but it is essential to be equally enthusiastic, equally sincere, at the end of the first week, and the end of the first month, and for all the months to come.

THE THREE STAGES OF MEDITATION

If the whole vista of the spiritual journey lay before us we would see that it divides into three stages, each culminating in a remarkable discovery. These are profound experiential discoveries, not intellectual ones. They bring a different way of seeing life and the power to make our words and deeds compatible with this new vision. Mere belief or theory is never enough; we must change ourselves. As one Christian mystic observed, "Our knowledge is as deep as our action."

Language cannot describe these inner experiences very well. When I say stages, I am only approximating. There are no sharp boundaries; everything takes place gradually over a long period. But perhaps a few analogies will make these discoveries easier to grasp.

In the first stage, we discover experientially that we are not the body.

Not the body? A startling realization! We have been lured into believing precisely the opposite: that we are *essentially* bodies, and that a worthwhile life is one well packed with sense-stimulation and pleasure, with all the delights of food and drink, sun and surf, luxurious fabrics and devastating fragrances.

What is the body then? Let me put it this way. I have a tan jacket of worsted wool made about ten years ago in Hong Kong. It fits me nicely, and I give it proper care: I don't drop it in a heap on a chair; I button it, smooth it out, and hang it up carefully in the closet so it will last several years more.

But when I wear this tan jacket, I always have another jacket on underneath: a brown one made in Kerala, India. It fits even better — not a seam anywhere — and has brown gloves to match. I take good care of it, too.

Now, you wouldn't confuse me with my tan woolen jacket, would you? Well, I have discovered after some years of meditation that this brown Kerala jacket, my body, is not me either, but simply something I wear. In fact, though you can't see me do it, I have learned how to take it off during meditation, leaving consciousness of the body behind. When meditation is over, I put it on again so that I may have the privilege of serving those around me. Someday my tan jacket will wear thin and have to be put aside. And someday too my brown jacket will no longer be useful for service, and I will have to put it aside in the great transformation we call death.

The discovery that you are not the body has far-reaching consequences. For one thing, you no longer see black or brown or white people, but people with all kinds of beautifully colored jackets. You no longer identify people with their color – or their age or sex or hairstyle or any other peripheral matter like money or status. You begin to awaken to the central truth of life, that all of us are one.

Then, too, you develop the capacity to see clearly the body's needs and how to provide for them wisely. You will not be taken in, for example, by just the taste of food, or by its color, or texture, or the sound it makes . . . or the sound the advertiser makes on its behalf. If the senses set up a clamor for junk food you can say affectionately, "Sorry, friends, that's not fit for you." The senses may be disappointed at first, of course, but your body will be grateful: "He really takes good care of me!"

Please do not think this means you lose your appreciation of food. Actually, it will increase. When you can change your eating habits at will, you not only enjoy wholesome food, you have the satisfaction of taking good care of your body. All the other things we charitably call food will leave you unsatisfied.

Wise choices in food, exercise, sleep – all these enhance your health. You feel vital, alive; fatigue leaves without saying goodbye. Minor ills like colds and flu will brush you lightly, if at all. Chronic complaints often dissolve, and you are largely shielded from many serious diseases like hypertension and heart disease. All this prolongs life and keeps you active, perhaps until the last day of this mortal life. In every tradition, sages often retain their vigor into their eighties and nineties.

In the first stage of meditation, then, we discover that our bodies are really garments we wear – or, if you like, vehicles in which we ride. After many years in this country, I have learned the ways of the automobile, and I feel comfortable with such a comparison. In the early days, though, I heard some expressions that confused me. Soon after I came to California I went on a trip with some friends. The lady driving suddenly announced with concern, "I'm out of water!" She looked all right to me – it hadn't been that long since we had eaten lunch – but I suggested she stop at the café ahead. Then someone explained, "She means the car is out of water." "Oh!" I said – thinking to myself, a little mystified, "Why doesn't she say that?"

All these bodies of ours are just cars moving about – some compacts, some big sedans. Some of them can dash away from a traffic light; others take a while to get going, especially in the morning. And although many were made in America, we have a refreshing mixture of imports too.

THE SECOND DISCOVERY

Having come to realize in the first stage of meditation that we are not our bodies, in the second stage we make an even more astounding discovery: we are not our minds either.

Sometimes when I state that, I catch the look on people's faces – a look that seems to say, "Just a minute! First, you tell us that we're not our bodies. Okay. Sounds craz— . . . well, *unusual*; but we're suspending judgment. But now you tell us with a straight face that we're not our minds either. My friend, you've just eliminated us completely!" When I see that look I hasten to add, "Wait a bit. There's more to the story."

If this body is like the body of a car, the mind is the engine — the most important part of the vehicle. As such, we ought to give it special attention and care. After all, you can get along with a Model T body if you have a Ferrari engine. But so many people who want a Ferrari body are content to keep an old Model T engine putt-putting along inside it. Most of their attention goes to externals: chrome hubcaps, bordeaux cherry vinyl seats, geodesic paint jobs, velveteen steering wheel covers, little dolls that shake their hula skirts in the back window. What is the good of all that if the pistons are worn out and your engine won't perform? We need minds that are powerful, lucid, capable of discrimination.

And we need minds that will follow directions, not ones that are rebellious. Suppose I come out one morning, start up my car, and drive off to give a talk on meditation in Milpitas, south of San Francisco. As soon as I cross the Golden Gate Bridge, my car veers east towards Interstate 80. I keep trying to turn the wheel, but there is tremendous resistance — the steering mechanism is ignoring me. "Milpitas!" I protest. "We're supposed to be going to Milpitas!" But the car only roars insolently, "Reno! Reno! We're going to Reno!" Then I think I hear it snicker, "Why not sit back and enjoy the ride?"

Would we put up with that? Well, no . . . not from our cars. But most of us do from our minds. In theory we would like the mind to listen to us obediently, but in fact it will not — chiefly because we have never taught it how. Augustine's words speak plainly: "I can tell my hand what to do and it will do it instantly. Why won't my mind do what I say?"

Everywhere there are a few people who will not accept this condition, who see it as a loss of freedom, a kind of bondage. My grandmother, my spiritual teacher, knew nothing about cars, but she understood the mind. When I would give tit-for-tat to others, wax angry because they were angry or standoffish because they stood off, she would say, "Son, when you act that way, you remind me of a rubber ball. Throw it against a wall and it *has* to come back." It took a while, but I finally resolved not to be a rubber ball in life.

I have often said that the spiritual life has nothing to do with the paranormal and the occult. But I do have one ability that seems to some people a kind of miracle, though it is simply a skill that anyone can develop through years of meditation: I can tell my mind what to do.

Where is the miracle? As Shakespeare's Hotspur would say, "Why, so can I, or so can any man." Well, here it is: when I tell my mind what to do, it obeys. If a craving should arise for something my body does not need, I smile and say politely, "Please leave," and it leaves. If something big tries to move in – say, an angry thought – I don't bandy words; I say plainly, "Out!" It goes immediately.

Meditation will do for you what it has done for all who practice it regularly: enable you to steer your car expertly. If you want to stay in one lane and cruise, your mind will obey you. If you want to change lanes or turn right or left or even make a U-turn, your mind will respond. When your mind does that at command, you have mastered the art of living. You are no longer dependent on external circumstances; you can decide how you want to respond, whatever happens. If a friend acts thoughtlessly, for example, you don't have to dwell on it; you can fix your attention on the good in that person instead. If you begin to feel low, you simply change your mind — you have learned how — and restore your equanimity and cheerfulness. You can now think what you want to think, and every relationship, everything you do, benefits enormously.

When you know you are not the body, you find it inaccurate to say, "I'm not feeling well." Your body may be indisposed, but you are always well. Now, in the second stage of meditation, you discover it equally inaccurate to say, "I am angry." The *mind* is angry. Instead of being consumed by anger, you can have a little fun at your own expense: "Hmm! There seems to be a nut loose up in there." A mechanical problem — anger — has developed, and if you know how to lie down on your mental car creeper, scoot under your mind, and tighten things up — or, more likely, loosen them a little — the problem can be set right. And you don't have to pay out hundreds of dollars before you get your car keys back.

This perspective brings precious distance — detachment — from the problems of both body and mind. For one, negative emotions no longer threaten. I mentioned anger, but fear comes under control as well. You can tune the engine of your mind very much the way you choose — in fact, you can come to have such mastery that even in your sleep, negative thoughts like resentment, hostility, and greed will not arise. You take full responsibility for your mental states as well as for your behavior.

A well-tuned mind helps to conserve the vital energy wasted in negative emotions. No one would leave a car running in the garage all night, but we let our minds run on much of the time.

No wonder we often feel tired and dispirited! This loss of vitality can even lead to illness.

Family and general practice physicians report that between seventy and eighty percent of their patients come in with psychologically generated complaints, vague feelings of "dis-ease." The Buddha had an incisive term for this: *duhkha,* which implies "out of joint." When vitality has been wasted we simply do not function well, like an elbow that has slipped out of place.

When we know how to set right any turmoil in the mind, all the power comes into our hands, to be used for the benefit of all. I cannot imagine a time when this was more essential. Every one of us has so much to give – more than we can realize – and it is so badly needed. Can we afford to waste it?

THE GREAT DISCOVERY

Having discovered that we are not the body, not the mind – both subject to change, to growth and decline – the question remains, "Who am I?" In the third stage, the tremendous climax of meditation, we make the most significant discovery any human being can ever make: we find out who we really are.

As long as we identify with the body and the mind we bob around on the surface level of consciousness, chasing after the fleeting attractions of life outside us. Here a pleasure won, there one lost. A bit of praise today, some criticism tomorrow. Profit, loss, profit, loss. Thus our days are spent, and we are scattered, divided, restless, incomplete.

Now, in profound meditation, we drop below all that and become concentrated on one thing and one thing alone: our true identity. In this absorption, this great gathering within, we break through the surface of consciousness and plummet deep, deep into our real nature.

What we discover cannot be put into words, but thereafter we are never again the same. With all our consciousness gathered to an intense focus within, the boundaries that seem to separate us from the rest of the world disappear. The duality of subject and object, knower and known, falls away; we are opened to a transcendental mode of knowing. Albert Einstein must have glimpsed this when he wrote from the perspective of a great physicist:

> A human being is a part of the whole, called by us "Universe," a part limited in time and space. He experiences himself, his thoughts and feelings as something separated from the rest — a kind of optical delusion of his consciousness. This delusion is a kind of prison for us, restricting us to our personal desires and to affection for a few persons nearest to us. Our task must be to free ourselves from this prison by widening our circle of compassion to embrace all living creatures and the whole of nature in its beauty.

In this profound state all petty personal longings, all hungering and thirsting, all sense of incompleteness vanish. We discover, almost in every cell of our being, that deep within us we lack nothing. Our inner reserves of love and wisdom are infinite; we can draw on them endlessly and never diminish them.

Previously, vague tones of discordancy sounded through what we thought and did. Like a shoe that pinches, a dislocated shoulder, the wrong key in a lock, matters were somehow just not right. But now a sense of rightness pervades our life; we fit, we belong.

This earth, nature, our fellow creatures, we ourselves — all things take their proper places in one grand harmony. Because we identify not with a fragment of life but with the whole, conflicts and division cease.

Of course, problems in the world remain — perhaps only now do we see just how threatening they really are. But we see too that they can be solved, and that we have the wisdom and resourcefulness with which to solve them. Those difficult stretches that test our mastery — sudden rises, hairpin turns, icy roads — we negotiate skillfully, like a practiced driver. And since we are fit to meet such challenges, they come — even big ones. But we stand ready: there will be difficult steering ahead, but we can manage it without fatigue or burnout.

Life itself becomes an effortless performance — very much like the virtuosity of a renowned pianist or cellist. The artist makes it look so easy; we almost want to exclaim, "Why, I could play that way!" But what enormous practice goes into such mastery! Once, it is said, a great painter took a mediocre portrait and brought it to vibrant life with a few quick strokes. His students were awed. "How did you manage to achieve that?" one asked. "It took just five minutes at most." The master said, "Oh, yes, it took only five minutes to do it. But it took twenty-five years to learn *how* to do it."

This skill in living brings beauty to your relationships. Only the sense of separateness makes us quarrelsome or difficult with others, and now no one can ever be separate from you again. Imagine that the little finger on your left hand turns feisty. It looks over at the thumb, which is minding its own business, and says, "What's that odd bird doing here? I'm going to tell him to clear out. If he doesn't, he's in for a drubbing!" What could be more absurd? Doesn't an injury to the thumb hurt the whole hand, of which the little finger is a member? When you discover your real nature, you discover simultaneously that you and others are one. In harming them, you are actually harming yourself; in being kind to them, you are being kind to yourself. All life is your family now, and though you express it in different ways with different people, you feel towards each person – to use the words of the Buddha – as a mother does towards her only child.

This does not mean that differences of opinion all vanish. There is diversity on the surface of life; that is what gives it interest. But now you always have the ability to understand other points of view. Aren't people essentially the same everywhere? The differences account for only one percent; the similarities, for ninety-nine. You can jump right out of your shoes or sandals into another's and see things as they do; you can leap right across supposed barriers of age, sex, economic status, nationality. You live in everybody, just as everybody lives in you.

Attaining this state of consciousness is the highest goal we can have in life. Different religions have called it by different names: illumination, enlightenment, nirvana, Self-realization, entering the promised land or the kingdom of heaven within. But whatever the language, the experience is everywhere the same. Jesus called it "a pearl of great price." Without it, our lives will always be wanting; even if we had to give everything on earth to obtain it, the cost would not be too high to pay.

If you set out on the path of meditation – and I certainly hope that you do – please follow carefully the guidelines presented here. Read them over and over until they become thoroughly familiar to you. You may have heard the expression, "When everything else fails, follow instructions." In meditation, you can avoid most difficulties by following the instructions from the very first. From my own experience, verified by the mystics of all lands, I know that in meditation we enter a new realm — or, more accurately, we enter with conscious eyes a realm that is already ours. To do this safely and surely we need guidance. These instructions are your guide.

You are now embarking on the most extraordinary journey, the most exacting and rewarding adventure, open to a man or woman. I haven't tried to conceal the fact that learning to control your mind is difficult — the most difficult thing in the world. But I want to remind you always that what you are seeking is glorious beyond compare, something far beyond my capacity, or anybody's, to render into thoughts and words. In my heart I have no greater desire than that you should reach the goal. Accept my wish for your great success!

Repetition of a Mantram

ON FESTIVAL DAYS in India you will often see a huge elephant, caparisoned in gold and gorgeous cloth, carrying an image of the Lord on its back through the village streets. Everyone enjoys the sight: the musicians with their drums and cymbals in front, then the beast slowly lumbering along and the devotees behind, all on their way to the temple.

But there can be one difficulty. Stalls of fruits, vegetables, and sweets line the narrow, crooked streets, and the trunk of an elephant, as you may know, rarely stays still. It sways back and forth, up and down, constantly. So when the procession comes abreast of a fruit stall, the elephant seizes a shelled coconut or two, opens his cavernous mouth, and tosses them in. At another stall the big fellow twists his trunk round a bunch of bananas suspended from the roof. The mouth opens again, the whole bunch goes in with a thud ... you hear a gulp ... and that's the end of it.

The humble people who own these stalls cannot afford this kind of loss, and to prevent it the man in charge, the mahout, asks the elephant to grasp a firm bamboo shaft in his trunk. Though not sure why, the elephant, out of love for his mahout, does as he is told. Now the procession can pass safely through the streets. The elephant steps right along with his stick held upright in a steady trunk, not tempted to feast on mangoes or melons because he has something to hold on to.

The human mind is rather like the trunk of an elephant. It never rests... it goes here, there, ceaselessly moving through sensations, images, thoughts, hopes, regrets, impulses. Occasionally it does solve a problem or make necessary plans, but most of the time it wanders at large, simply because we do not know how to keep it quiet or profitably engaged.

But what should we give it to hold on to? For this purpose I recommend the systematic repetition of the mantram, which can steady the mind at any time and in any place.

WHAT IS A MANTRAM?

Of late, the ancient word *mantram* (or the familiar variant *mantra*) has had considerable exposure on talk shows and in the Sunday supplements. To many it may conjure up an exotic image of flowing robes, garlands, and incense. It may seem to be something impractical and otherworldly, perhaps a bit magical and mysterious. Actually, just the opposite holds true. The mantram — under other names, to be sure — has been known in the West for centuries, and there need not be anything secret or occult about it. The mantram stands open to all. And since it can calm our hearts and minds, it is about as practical as anything can be.

If you have preconceptions about using a mantram, let me ask you to put them aside and give it a personal trial. Why take someone else's word for it? Enter the laboratory of your mind and perform the experiment. Then you will be in a position to judge for yourself, and nothing can be as persuasive as that.

A mantram is a spiritual formula of enormous power that has been transmitted from age to age in a religious tradition. The users, wishing to draw upon this power that calms and heals, silently repeat the words as often as possible during the day, each repetition adding to their physical and spiritual well-being. In a sense, that is all there is to a mantram. In another sense, there is so much! Those who have tried it — saints, sages, and ordinary people too — know from their own experience its marvelous potency.

We find a clue to the workings of the mantram in the popular etymology which links the word to the roots *man,* "the mind," and *tri,* "to cross." The mantram, repeated regularly for a long time, enables us to cross the sea of the mind.

An apt image, for the mind very much resembles a sea. Ever-changing, it is placid one day, turbulent the next. Awesome creatures lurk below in the unconscious — fears and animosities, desires and conflicts. Each of us drifts about on the surface, blown by typhoons and carried by currents, in a rudderless little boat called "I." With such vast and treacherous waters before us, with no glimpse at all of the far shore, can we ever hope to make the crossing without some help?

The mantram is such help. The scriptures of all religions proclaim it to be a radiant symbol of ultimate existence, the supreme reality which, depending on our background, we call by various expressive names: God, Nature, the Divine Mother, the Clear Light, universal consciousness. What we call it matters little. What matters greatly is that we discover — experientially, not intellectually — that this supreme reality rests at the inmost center of our being. This discovery constitutes the goal of life, and the mantram stands as a perpetual reminder that such perfection is within all of us, waiting to flow through our thoughts, words, and deeds.

WHAT THE MANTRAM CAN DO

In the simple act of repeating the mantram we accomplish remarkable things. The tension in our bodies, the cause of specific complaints and general malaise, ebbs away, and we find delightfully that real health is more than just an absence of disease. We toughen our will, too, which signals the end of addictions that may have enslaved us for years. Internal divisions are healed and our purposes unified, so we become a beneficent force in life and not, as all of us may have been at times, something of a burden on the earth. We gain access to inner resources — courage, patience, compassion — which are presently locked up within. Then all our relationships flourish; we love and are loved. Gradually, if we repeat it often, the mantram permeates and utterly transforms our consciousness.

This is a strong claim. Can a mere word achieve all that? It is a natural question. I remember when I had to give a speech to my high school class; I was so nervous at the prospect that I was afraid my knees might not hold me up. My spiritual teacher said, "While you're waiting for your turn, don't sit there worrying about the audience; repeat the mantram." I was skeptical, but because I loved her I did as she suggested. I remember saying to myself, "*Rama, Rama, Rama*...I hope it works."

I got through the ordeal safely enough, so the next time I had to give a speech I tried the mantram again...and again. I soon found myself saying, "*Rama, Rama*...I think it works!" Now, after many years of practice, I *know* it works. As a medical friend once told me, until recently we didn't know how aspirin works, but that didn't keep it from relieving pain. Similarly, with the mantram, no explanation I can give can take the place of your own personal verification.

In daily life we often credit even common words with immense power. Take advertising. Be it soup or soap, cereal or cigarettes, product makers understand the impact of words and spend millions yearly trying to lodge a jingle, slogan, or brand name in our minds. And the key element of the campaign is repetition.

All that pounding away harms us because we are induced to buy things we don't need, things that may weaken our bodies. But why can't we use the obvious effectiveness of such repetition for our health and peace of mind? When we repeat a mantram, that is precisely what we do.

Repeating a mantram sounds so simple that most people cannot believe it works until they try it. For one thing, many consider it mere mechanical repetition — a job for any voice recorder. But I would say that a journey makes a better analogy. Each step on a journey superficially resembles the others, but each uniquely takes you into new territory and moves you closer to your destination. In just the same way, the repetitions of the mantram are superficially alike, but each takes you ever deeper into consciousness and closer to the goal of love and joyful awareness.

Mystics East and West have answered this objection. Mahatma Gandhi wrote:

> The mantram becomes one's staff of life and carries one through every ordeal. It is not repeated for the sake of repetition, but for the sake of purification, as an aid to

effort. It is no empty repetition. For each repetition has a new meaning, carrying you nearer and nearer to God.

And in *The Way of a Pilgrim,* the remarkable tale of a Russian peasant's spiritual pilgrimage, we read:

Many so-called enlightened people regard this frequent offering of one and the same prayer as useless and even trifling, calling it mechanical and a thoughtless occupation of simple people. But unfortunately they do not know the secret which is revealed as a result of this mechanical exercise; they do not know how this frequent service of the lips imperceptibly becomes a genuine appeal of the heart, sinks down into the inward life, becomes a delight — becomes, as it were, natural to the soul, bringing it light and nourishment and leading it on to union with God.

Nor can we call the mantram mere reverie or self-hypnosis — an attempt to escape from problems, whether personal, social, or global. When we are refashioning our consciousness so that what is ruinous in us becomes creative, our actions cannot help adding to the welfare of the whole. Our sensitivity grows until we become quite incapable of thinking of our own needs in isolation from the rest of life.

THE MANTRAM AND MEDITATION

In the program presented in this book, the use of a mantram is distinct from meditation. You have to sit down to meditate, close your eyes, and repeat the inspirational passage for a certain period of time. You can't practice meditation while you are walking or waiting in a queue. Nor can you resort to it on the spot if someone aims an unkind remark at you, or if you find yourself besieged by an old temptation.

The mantram, on the other hand, can be repeated anywhere and at any time. And while meditation demands discipline and will, the mantram requires only the effort needed to start it up and keep it going. What matters is saying it; as long as you do that, the healing work goes on.

Meditation, to put it playfully, is like placing a call to the Lord on your own phone. You can talk, but you must work hard every day to earn the money to pay for the account. But even if you have no money, you can always call collect. Just say, "Lord, I'm broke – not a cent to my name to pay for this call – but I'm really desperate!" If you keep calling the Lord through the mantram, he'll finally say out of infinite love, "Yes, I see your situation. You can count on me." After all, you are not calling on anybody outside you. The Lord is your real Self, and when you use the mantram to call on him within you, it releases deep inner resources.

The mantram fits everybody. It does not matter where you live, what you do, or how old you are. Whether you have four degrees or never went to school at all, whether you are rich, poor, or something in between, whether you are sick or well, you can use the mantram.

SOME GREAT MANTRAMS

Because the mantram is, above all, a spiritual tool to be used, I am going to skirt around its more technical aspects. You can come across some very erudite theories that link mantrams to the basic vibrations of matter and energy in the universe, but here our focus will be on a method for changing lives, not on speculation. I admire the impulse, common in this country, which leads someone to listen for a while to theory and then say, "Okay, when do we start?"

Let us begin by looking at some of the great mantrams that have come down to us. You will find them in all the religions of the world – itself a testimony to their universal appeal and proven worth.

In Christianity, the mantram is often called the holy name. Indeed, the very name of Jesus constitutes a mantram that can be repeated – *Jesus, Jesus* – by anyone who yearns to become more like Christ, full of wisdom, mercy, and love. In the Orthodox Church, the Jesus Prayer – *Lord Jesus Christ, Son of God, have mercy on us* – has been used in this way for centuries. Shorter versions, such as *Lord Jesus Christ* or *Kyrie eleison,* are also found.

Catholics who have been saying *Hail Mary* or *Ave Maria* regularly for years may be surprised to hear that they already have a mantram – a bit like the character in Molière's play who discovers that he has always been speaking prose. In India we say that a mother will busy herself at the stove while her child plays happily in the next room. But when the child grows tired of toys, throws them down, and begins to cry, the mother immediately comes in to give comfort. So, too, when we stop playing with our adult toys and call out for Mother Mary, she will come to our rescue from within.

Jews may use the ancient *Barukh attah Adonai,* "Blessed art thou, O Lord," or *Ribono shel olam,* "Lord of the universe," which I am told has been used continuously by Hasidic mystics for almost two hundred years. In Islam, *Allahu akbar* — "God is great" — remains one of the most popular mantrams. Other popular choices are *Bismillah ir-Rahman ir-Rahim,* "In the name of God, the Merciful, the Compassionate," or simply *Allah, Allah.*

Om mani padme hum, used by Buddhists for centuries, signifies "the jewel in the lotus of the heart" — a reference to the hidden spark of divinity within each human being. Here the heart is likened to the lotus, a symbol as universal in the East as the rose is in the West. The lotus takes root in the mud at the bottom of a pond and sends its tall stalk up through the water towards the light. At last it breaks into the clear air, the leaves resting on the surface, the blossom opening to the sun and following it throughout the day. We are thus reminded that however imperfect our beginnings, whatever mistakes we may have made in the past, all of us can purify our hearts and come to dwell in spiritual illumination.

Of the many mantrams from India, one of the most powerful is the simple *Rama.* This was Mahatma Gandhi's mantram; with it he transformed himself from an ineffective lawyer into the irresistible force that won his country's freedom, not with bullets, not with hate, but with truth and love — *Rama* comes from a Sanskrit root meaning "to rejoice." Anyone who repeats it summons the great joy found in our deepest Self.

Rama also forms the core of the mantram I heard so many times from my own spiritual teacher as she went about her daily chores, milking the cows or sweeping the courtyard with a coconut-fiber broom. I think that is the sweetest sound I have ever heard, and it echoes in my consciousness strongly still:

Hare Rama Hare Rama
Rama Rama Hare Hare
Hare Krishna Hare Krishna
Krishna Krishna Hare Hare

This mantram consists of three holy names. *Hare* (pronounced *ha-ray*) is a name for God derived from the Sanskrit *har,* "to steal." What bold imagery! The Lord may be tagged the Divine Thief because he has stolen our hearts, and we cannot rest until we catch him. *Rama,* as we have seen, represents the Lord as the source of all joy. And *Krishna* comes from the root *karsh,* "to draw" — he who ceaselessly, ceaselessly draws us to himself.

These are some of the most widely used and best-loved mantrams from the major religions of the world. Clearly, when you decide to use a mantram, you are not taking up a practice that has, as we say in my mother tongue, "sprung up like last night's mushrooms." The repetition of the mantram is venerable, universal, proven. It has been verified by the experience of millions of men and women everywhere, in every age. True, mantrams have different sounds and come from diverse traditions. But essentially they all do the same thing: turn us away from our dependency on what lies outside — money and things, awards and position, pleasure and comfort, selfish relationships and power — to the serenity and goodness within our own being.

CHOOSING A MANTRAM

Please exercise some care in your choice of a mantram. After all, it will be with you for a long time. Deliberate for a while and take into account the practical significance of the words, your religious background, and your personal response. A bit of self-knowledge is required when it comes to making a selection. Some people respond profoundly to the Virgin Mary, and *Hail Mary* may be the mantram for them. Or perhaps her holy son touches them deeply, and *Jesus, Jesus* will be their choice. But other people, owing to the conditioning of their youth, have a kind of allergy to certain names, sometimes the ones from their own religious traditions. When people tell me they do not care for a particular holy name, I simply encourage them to choose something else. That's plain economy. It will take a long while to become established in the mantram; is there time to spend a couple of years just learning to like it?

If you have such negative associations from childhood, you might choose *Rama*. Easy to say, sonorous, it embodies a principle – the principle of joy – that everybody, irrespective of background, can appreciate. I also recommend *Om mani padme hum* to those with reservations about the holy name. This mantram, associated with the Compassionate Buddha, does not refer to God at all. The Buddha's approach is free of ritual, theology, and dogma, full of empirical examination. He does not indulge in metaphysical speculation; he simply says, "Here is the boat; there lies the goal, the opposite shore. Don't take my word for what you will find there; go and find out for yourselves."

Initially, the mantram you have chosen may not sound natural to your ears. But I assure you this will soon pass. After a little while the mantram will "take," and you will see for yourself the difference it makes in your life. These matters go beyond the diversity of languages, and your higher Self, your true Self, will not care whether you speak to it in English, Arabic, Latin, or Sanskrit.

Occasionally someone will ask, "Can I make up my own mantram? How about 'Peace'?" *Peace* is a beautiful word, I know, but not any word will do as a mantram. I strongly urge you to choose a mantram that has been sanctified by long use – one of proven power, that has enabled many men and women before you to realize the unity of life. The roots of such a mantram go far deeper than we can ever know when we begin to use it. This profundity enables it to grow in our consciousness.

After you have chosen your mantram carefully, please do not change it under any circumstances. Many people let themselves be swept away by novelty; it is part of the restlessness of our age. They will use a mantram for six weeks and then tire of it. They change to another, and then grow weary of that one too. So they go on in this way, new mantram after new, like a farmer who keeps starting a new well; they will never find water.

Let me urge you not to yield to the temptation to change your mantram if you do not seem to be getting anywhere, as may happen from time to time. That is only a trick of the wily mind to throw you off – usually because you *are* getting somewhere, and the mind knows it. No matter what comes up that seems newer and better, keep digging away with your chosen mantram. One day you *will* strike the living waters!

HOW TO REPEAT THE MANTRAM

The mantram works best when we repeat it silently in the mind with as much concentration as possible. Mantrams are usually rhythmical, but if you sing or chant them it will draw your attention towards the tune or rhythm and away from the mantram itself. Saying your mantram a few times out loud may help you get it going in your mind, but by and large I encourage you to stick to a silent repetition.

And you need not concern yourself with finding just the "right" pronunciation or intonation when you say your mantram. If the Lord will listen to you in any language, he will certainly accept your accent, wherever you are from. Above all, it is the calling that counts, and we want to focus on that and on nothing peripheral.

Our aim, remember, is to drive the mantram to the deepest levels of consciousness, where it operates not as words but as a healing power. So avoid anything that holds you to the surface level; otherwise, you are in the position of someone trying to dive to the bottom of a lake while wearing water wings. For this reason, I do not recommend counting your repetitions or using manual aids like a rosary. Though these things may seem helpful at the start, keeping track of numbers or remembering what your hands are doing binds you to the physical level and can lead to a merely mechanical repetition.

Trying to synchronize your mantram with physiological processes, such as heartbeat or breathing, also divides your attention. No harm will result if this happens by itself, but do not try to make the connection. Actually, it can be quite hazardous to interfere with vital functions that are already operating smoothly without our conscious intervention.

USE EVERY OPPORTUNITY

The purpose of having a mantram is to repeat it as often as possible. Beautiful calligraphy of the words for your wall is not enough; you have to set about making the mantram an integral part of all your responses, all your thoughts and feelings. And you have to persist. If you do it for just a few minutes and then lose heart, little will be gained.

Sometimes you hear that it is essential to repeat a mantram a certain number of times or for a specified period of time. Perhaps some spiritual teachers living in the monastic context have required that of their students, but where are we who live in the world going to find an hour or two of uninterrupted time for repeating the mantram? You might manage that if you work the graveyard shift at a toll bridge, or if you have a role in a movie where they need a couple of hours to put on your makeup, but most of us are going to have to catch as catch can.

Over the years I have learned to use every opportunity, no matter how brief, to repeat the mantram. We can take advantage of all the odds and ends of time that present themselves during the day, and even set out to find them, as a miser scans the sidewalk for a coin that has chanced to fall from someone's pocket. We all come upon these little bits of time, you know, but most of us fail to seize them. Look at the people at bus stops at a loss for what to do! Some tug their ear lobes or work their knuckles; some vacantly watch the cars drive by or read a billboard for the eleventh time. Others keep rising to see if the bus is coming, as if that would bring it any sooner. And just watch people at a theater intermission as they rush out to have a cigarette or to eat food they don't need!

Actually, many injurious habits result from our efforts to fill empty time. Considering the health risks in smoking and overeating, imagine how people must dread having nothing to do and what price they will pay to avoid it. The mantram ends this dread permanently.

Two minutes here…five minutes there…all those snatches of time add up. On the Blue Mountain in India, where I lived, the villagers lacked the means for traveling to town, so the small bank sent a boy around to the cottages every day on a bicycle to ask if anybody wanted to make a deposit. Usually there would only be a few small coins, but all was carefully recorded, and at the end of the year someone might have amassed fifty or a hundred rupees. That is how the mantram works. It accumulates and accumulates, finally paying a far richer dividend than any bank ever can.

The mantram also proves to be an absorbing companion when we are doing mechanical tasks. All of us have chores which don't require concentration – cleaning the house or shop, washing the car or the dishes, brushing hair, brushing teeth – and most of our attention flies elsewhere, commonly to the future or past. All that excess mental power can be put behind the mantram, so that as we clean things, we clean our consciousness as well.

But do distinguish such mechanical tasks from activities that require concentration. When listening to music or lectures, when reading, writing, studying, or conversing with others, it is good to be fully attentive. These are not times for repeating the mantram.

I have observed that many people treat driving as automatic. But lives are at stake, and to avoid accidents we must be supremely vigilant. Even in light traffic the unexpected can happen: a tire goes flat, an animal or child darts onto the road. So please do not repeat the mantram at the wheel. When operating any kind of powerful machinery, or when using dangerous tools like chisels or kitchen knives, concentrate on the job at hand.

It is refreshing to close one's eyes and repeat the mantram

silently a few times before each meal — a reminder that food comes to us as a gift from the Lord, a precious gift of energy to be used wisely. If you eat lunch on the job, the mantram also brings detachment, the ability to drop your work and enjoy the meal in front of you. In fact, you might stop briefly to repeat the mantram and draw yourself out of your involvement several times during the day. If you are doing close work — reading, typing, sewing, or small repair jobs — you can use this moment to rest your eyes by shifting your gaze into the far distance.

Carry the mantram along when you step out for your daily exercise, too. Energetic movement is not an option, not a luxury, but an imperative on the spiritual path if we are to do the work that needs doing. Young people require strenuous activities, such as jogging, swimming, and hard work, that tax the heart and lungs. And nearly all of us, of course, can walk, as briskly as our condition permits. I say "briskly" because the body is designed for and thrives on vigorous motion, so give it a pace that will send the blood spinning through the veins and bring the cells to life. And as you exercise, repeat the mantram; you will be regenerating your mind as well as your body.

Here again, you should not wait until you come upon a full free hour; perhaps it will never happen. Use the time you have, five or ten or fifteen minutes. Instead of coffee or a snack, try a mantram break. To the store or bank, at the beach or park, up and down stairs, wherever you can, move with your mantram.

AT NIGHT

Above all, use the mantram as a preparation for sleep. Few of us realize the impact of what goes on in our minds at night. "Oh," we say, "I have *some* dreams, but I don't remember them very well." They seem no more substantial than movies seen years ago, and we dismiss the matter. Actually, there is a vast newsroom in our deeper consciousness that starts to hum just before we fall asleep as everyone prepares for the night edition. Reporters rush hot items — the events of the day — to the city desk. One Pulitzer Prize winner pounds out a special piece on resentment; he has been working on it all day and filled up quite a sheaf of pages. Another reporter calls with a "stop press" — he has some fears about tomorrow, big ones, that simply must go in. So the edition is "put to bed" right there in your bed, and it appears as dreams. An extra, a really sensational edition with giant headlines, that's a nightmare.

All the turmoil of the day rises in our minds as we loosen conscious control, and it continues on into sleep. As a result, we don't rest very well. Haven't you ever got up unrefreshed, almost as tired as when you lay down? And when we read agitating books and magazines or watch violent television shows and movies before we go to bed, we make it much worse.

That is why I recommend that you read some spiritual literature before you turn out the light. I will suggest specific material in a later chapter, but I want to stress now the connection between what you do before going to sleep and the contents of sleep itself. After you have finished your reading, close your eyes and start repeating your mantram silently — *Rama, Rama, Rama* or *Jesus, Jesus* — until you fall asleep saying it.

This is not as easy as it sounds. You will have to practice it for a while, and you will have to exert some effort. At the beginning, it may even keep you wakeful for a time. People have complained that they lose an hour's sleep repeating the mantram. I don't think that constitutes a crisis, and I usually reply, "Congratulations! While you're learning to fall asleep in it, you are getting an extra hour of repetition."

If you keep practicing this skill, your entire attitude towards sleep will change. Have you ever seen youngsters stand at the foot of their beds and fling themselves backwards onto the mattress without even looking? No broken bones, no broken beds – they are sure of themselves, and it all works out. When you have learned to fall asleep in the mantram, you too will be sure that everything is well as you near your bed. There will be no anxiety about what lies ahead: will I sleep or thrash about, or have nightmares, or wake up tired – or fail to wake up at all? The mantram is the ideal tranquilizer, and it leads to a full night of restorative sleep.

Between the last waking moment and the first sleeping moment, a tunnel stretches down deep into consciousness. Most people do not perceive this subtle state; indeed, you cannot be aware of it with your everyday mind. At that instant, when you are neither awake nor asleep, this tunnel opens up, and if you know how, you can send the mantram down it as you might a bowling ball. The proof is that you may hear the mantram during sleep; when an unpleasant dream begins, you may discover the mantram echoing through consciousness, dissolving that dream completely. A profound and peaceful sleep comes to you, so you wake up in the morning refreshed in body, calm in mind, and strong in your faith in the mantram's power.

DEALING WITH EMOTIONS

In one other context the mantram is of inestimable help—when negative emotions sweep through our minds. We make a remark, for instance, and someone suddenly fires back a verbal fusillade. The normal response would be to speak even more discourteously in return—which, of course, only provokes the other person to retaliate. This can go on, insults flying about, until one party breaks something or starts packing a suitcase.

Instead of getting caught in this destructive game of tit-for-tat, repeat the mantram. If you can, leave—gracefully if possible, ungracefully if not—and go for a long, brisk walk repeating your mantram. Leave as soon as you become aware that you are about to get entangled. Don't try for one final cutting remark, one last clever double entendre; go outside and begin your mantram walk.

You will have more than just the mantram working for you. The rhythm of the words will soon be reinforced by the rhythm of your footsteps—and, as the anger subsides, by the rhythm of your breathing and heartbeat too. In this harmony your mind will gradually grow calmer and you will gain the precious detachment you need to understand the quarrel clearly. Gradually you will see the other person's point of view—perhaps you will realize the stress he is under, or how her conditioning has shaped her attitudes—and hostility will give way to compassion.

It may take a while for anger to be transformed on such a walk—half an hour, an hour, or even longer. But isn't that a sound investment of your time? You might well waste that much or more in enlarging the conflict, and still more in seething with resentment. But now you return with a measure of sympathy, able to bring the estrangement to an end. Often the other person will see the change and respond. Deep inside, he or she too has been suffering acutely at the rupture between you.

Psychologically-minded people sometimes ask, "Aren't you advocating a kind of unhealthy suppression?" As I understand it, in suppression we force a wave of, say, anger below the surface level, where it acts destructively on our own bodies. Today we are assured that we do better to let negative emotions gush forth, however painful this may be for those around us, than to let them build up and stagnate within. But the mantram provides a third alternative. The tremendous power behind these emotions can be rechanneled, put to work to calm the mind and to conciliate differences. The power is there in both cases, but now it works for us rather than against us.

Like a skilled trainer, the mantram harnesses restlessness. We live in an era of hectic movement, of going places, of shifting from job to job, house to house. When I see marked restlessness in people, though, I am hopeful, because I know they possess the energy they need for spiritual growth. But they cannot grow if they continually drive off to see the sights, or window-shop, or drop in at the spots where, supposedly, the action is. All of that depletes vitality and gives us nothing to show for it. If you ever feel such restlessness – or the mental kind that leads to compulsive talking, reading, and TV-watching – take a mantram walk or write your mantram a fixed number of times, say, a hundred or more. In this way, your vital energy will be consolidated and will not ebb out.

UPS AND DOWNS

Extreme oscillations of the mind like elation and depression — not severe clinical depression, but those all-too-familiar mood slumps that bleach the color out of life — can be controlled by the mantram. You will find excitement played up everywhere today — thrilling flavors, intoxicatingly new eye shadow, vans with breathtaking accessories — and everywhere today you will find depressed people. Hardly anyone sees a connection. Hardly anyone realizes that the old truth "What goes up must come down" applies to the mind too. We believe that we should pursue excitement as much as possible and that if we are lucky we can have it all the time. If we are unlucky — well, we can have a drink or take a pill and try again later.

This whole problem is a large and complex one, and I have dealt with it at length in a companion volume, *The Mantram Handbook*. Let me just say here that in our behavior, we often defy an inescapable principle: if you let your mind be ruffled by what is pleasant, it is bound to be ruffled by what is unpleasant. Outwardly, the slump and downturned gaze of someone down-in-the-dumps seem far from the giddy gestures and chatter of the elated person, but in both cases the mind has gone out of control.

In other words, excitement makes us vulnerable to depression. When I say this, you may think that I am trying to wrap a wet blanket around you. But actually, when we reduce the pendulum swings of the mind, we enter a calm state of awareness that allows us to enjoy the present moment most fully.

Whenever you find disappointment starting to drag you down, use the mantram to pull yourself back again. But more important, learn to prevent low moods altogether by repeating your mantram when you first feel yourself becoming excited. When praise comes, for instance, don't let yourself be swept away by it. If you do, you will as surely be swept away by the criticism that life inevitably brings. When you find yourself dwelling on future events – the party tonight, your next vacation, graduation, retirement – bring yourself back to the present moment so you can avoid disappointment if future events take an unexpected turn. Above all, use the mantram to free yourself from the tyranny of strong likes and dislikes – all those preferences, aversions, fixed opinions, and habits that make us soar when things go our way and crash when they do not. The mantram can free us from all dependence on outer events, so that we can remain cheerful whatever happens.

IN TIMES OF CRISIS

The mantram works beautifully also when fear and worry invade us. During my first year in this country I became good friends with the handful of students from India who were attending the University of Minnesota. One afternoon a very bright chap told me he had a final in physics the next morning and was sure he would fail. I asked him if he had been studying right along. "Yes," he said, "but I know I'm going to forget everything at the critical moment." He wrung his hands and looked most miserable, a Romeo throwing himself down in Friar Lawrence's cell and crying out that all was lost.

It was a frigid day, snow blanketing everything, and most Indians are not at all fond of cold. But this called for immediate action. "Get your coat, please," I said, "and start repeating your mantram. We're going out."

We did. From time to time he wanted to bring up the matter of his impending failure, but I just said, "Don't talk. Repeat the mantram." On and on we walked, from Minneapolis to St. Paul and back again, a distance of about twelve miles. When we got back that night I led him up to the dorm, opened his door, gave him a loving push, and he dropped on the bed so completely relaxed that he fell asleep instantly. I made sure that there was someone to get him up on time, and left. Of course, he did splendidly on the exam.

The mantram took care of his anxiety, but it didn't put any physics formulae in his head. Hard study did that. You can't spend an entire semester playing chess or chatting in the campus co-op and then expect the mantram to rescue you. Similarly, when it comes to travel, the mantram cannot take the place of good tires and properly adjusted brakes. But if you have done all you can, then the mantram can free you from energy-sapping, pointless fear.

Children often suffer from little fears, and they too can use the mantram to mitigate them. When they wake up from a nightmare, for instance, we can comfort them and then suggest they repeat the mantram. Divine figures like Krishna and baby Jesus appeal to the young; so they can often learn to say the mantram at an early age. It is not good to be insistent about such things, of course; choose the right time and the right degree of exposure. But even preschoolers can take easily to repeating the mantram before meals and when they are afraid.

The mantram disposes of painful memories, which prowl through the mind, abducting us into the past. When these apparitions appear — resentments, missed opportunities, rejections — we can render them powerless. If they come at night, their favorite time, drive them away with the mantram. Eventually you can reach such a secure state that you can say to these fellows, "I'll give you five minutes. Go ahead and put on your show." And the Guardian of the Tomb of Time looks at you through his empty sockets, rattles his keys and chains, and opens the crypt door. The memory of a sweetheart leaving you crawls forth, and there it is...the same tired performance. Instead of getting agitated and reaching for a drink or a pill or a piece of chocolate cake, you sit there and watch. At the end, you applaud and call out, "Well done, you old fraud!" And the memory, terribly disappointed that it couldn't upset you, leaves, never to be heard from again.

When pain comes, as it must to all, the mantram gives the mind something to hang on to. It is especially helpful during illness – particularly for those who have been hospitalized, who often feel anxious and even angry as they lie in an intensive care unit or wait to be wheeled into major surgery. Instead of repeating "Pain...pain...," adding mental anguish to physical, why not say *Jesus, Jesus* or *Rama, Rama* and cast ourselves into the arms of one who transcends all suffering? I would not hesitate to offer the mantram in such circumstances, even to agnostics. True, such people may not believe in God. But if you are dear to them, they may be willing to try something that helps, though they don't understand how or why it works.

In the midst of any powerful emotion like fear or anger, you may find it difficult to hold on to the mantram if it is a long one. In such emergencies I suggest you repeat a shortened form based on the most potent word: *Rama* if you use *Hare Rama, Hare Rama* or *Jesus* if you use the Jesus Prayer. When you are greatly agitated, it will be easier to stay with this kernel word.

THE MANTRAM REPEATING ITSELF

Naturally, skill at holding on to the mantram increases with practice. In the early days the mind is out of shape, and its flabby fingers won't close tightly. The grip feels tentative, modest. In time, however, its fingers grow stronger and the mind can grasp firmly, though occasionally the mantram still slips away. After a long while, the mind builds up sensational strength and has a permanent hold on the mantram.

In this glorious state, the mantram repeats itself ceaselessly without any effort whatsoever. Walking along a road, waiting for a friend, dropping off to sleep, you will hear the mantram tolling through consciousness. If you're fully absorbed in some activity—at a concert, for instance—the mantram repeats itself on a deeper level. Then, when the intermission begins the mantram rises and resounds on the surface level as well.

Sanskrit has a precise word for this state: *ajapajapam*. *Japam* alone means the repetition of the mantram, and *a* here means "without": *ajapajapam* is *japam* without having to do *japam*. You receive all the benefits without having to do the work. There is nothing magical or occult in this. It results from the steadfast practice of repeating the mantram at every possible moment for many, many years. This state may be likened to that of a person retiring from his career. For decades he has had to be at the office faithfully, and sometimes it may have taken a lot of effort. But now the harvest has been gathered—he draws a pension without having to report ever again.

At this stage, the mystics say, the Lord himself is present, pleased to utter his own name as a perpetual blessing on a devoted servant. Great waves of joy sweep through such a man or woman, and a divine radiance touches everything. Meister Eckhart spoke of this more than six hundred years ago:

> Those who have God in mind, simply and solely God in all things, carry God with them into all their works and into all places, and God alone does all their works. They see nothing but God; nothing seems good to them but God. They become one with God in every thought. Just as no multiplicity can dissipate God, so nothing can dissipate them or make them multiple.

Slowing Down

WHEN I CAME to America on the Fulbright exchange program many years ago, my friends warned me about the pace of life I would find here. I had never been out of India and was used to the leisurely gait of the village, so I listened politely but without much understanding.

I sailed the Atlantic and arrived in New York City – I just couldn't believe my eyes! As I stepped from the harbor into the city, I saw people with briefcases and bulky shopping bags scurrying along the sidewalks. Men were pushing huge racks of clothes on wheels and dragging carts of food through the streets, and everyone seemed to be in a terrible hurry.

A few days later I experienced a freeway for the first time, and again I was stunned. The cars tore by, and for a moment I thought there must be a race in progress. I couldn't imagine why all those people were going sixty or seventy miles per hour. I had to admit, sadly, that my friends in India certainly knew what they were talking about.

I then made my first decision in this country: no one is going to make me run. I will walk, I said to myself, at the same old bullock cart pace of three miles per hour – in an emergency, four.

I will keep the sensible and life-prolonging pace that prevails in the rural areas around the world. I have maintained it ever since, and I believe too that I've acted as a bit of a brake on the speed of those around me.

People say that modern life has grown so complicated, so busy, so crowded that we have to hurry even to survive. We need not accept that idea. It is quite possible to live in the midst of a highly developed technological society and keep an easy, relaxed pace while doing a lot of hard work. We have a choice. We are not mere victims of our environment, and we don't have to go fast just because everybody else does and urges us to do it too.

Often we may not even be aware that we are hurrying. If we have lived that way all our life and been around people who hurry, it is difficult for us to see how fast everything moves. What can we compare it to? Speed becomes a habit we do not know we have. I'm told that people who live next to freeways no longer hear the cars, and perhaps you have had the same experience around a piece of noisy machinery. Rushing about is very much like that.

Initially, our bodies do the speeding under our conscious direction. We run down the stairs, bolt into rooms, slam doors – it is mainly physical. But after a while we become habituated to going faster and faster, and speed gradually takes over the mind. A kind of compulsive pressure builds up. Now we really have a problem, because it is very hard to change such a pattern of living. Just as an eye cannot observe its own working, so a rapid mind cannot take the time to perceive its own rapidity.

When the mind starts whirring in this way, a person easily loses control of his thoughts and actions. My wife and I once went into a café in San Francisco during the lunch hour, and the people working there were in such a flurry that one nearly hit the head of the fellow next to me with a plate. She hadn't lost her temper, she had no grievance against him, but the sheer speed of her movement so unnerved her that the plate flew out of her hands. A great deal of carelessness results from hurry, and all kinds of accidents that we choose to call chance or fate or luck are actually simple processes of cause and effect. We do not see the causal connections because we move too fast to notice.

Speeded-up people can be likened to automata, to robots. Perhaps you remember that insightful Chaplin movie *Modern Times*? Charlie stands at an assembly line in a factory, and for eight hours a day he tightens a nut with his wrench as each piece goes by. From time to time the boss turns up the pace of the conveyor belt, and poor Charlie has to work even faster. Throughout the day he makes the same movement with his arm. When he comes out after eight hours, he cannot stop. Though he has no wrench, he makes the same gesture all the way home, to the amazement of the passersby.

This is what happens to speeded-up people. They become automatic, which means they have no freedom and no choices, only compulsions. Since they take no time to reflect on things, they gradually lose the capacity for reflection. Without reflection, how can we change? We first have to be able to sit back, examine ourselves with detachment, and search out our patterns of behavior. Paradoxically, people who hurry are actually stuck in the same spot.

SLOWNESS AND SENSITIVITY

When we go faster and faster, we grow more and more insensitive to the needs of everyone around. We become dull, blunted, imperceptive. In the morning, for instance, when we are moving like a launched missile, our vigilance falls; we may hurt the feelings of our children or partner and never know it at all. To be aware of others, we have to go slowly and pay attention to what is happening. Our faculties must be alert and fully functioning.

Sometimes, under the goad of speed, we act as if other people are not there. When we move fast, those around us seem to be blurs, like statues glimpsed through the fog. Our minds are elsewhere, and we have just enough attention in the present moment to avoid knocking everybody down – and sometimes not even that much! We will shove our way in front of others when they are reaching for something, squeeze by them at the door, shut the lights out on them when we leave the room, disturb them by talking out loud to ourselves or whistling or banging things about – and all this because we do not truly see them. We are caught in this relentless pattern of rushing, and around and around we go, with our faces grimly set and our eyes vacant. Not a pretty picture, but one we can change, and change completely.

We need to remember, too, that hurry is contagious. When a person comes rushing into a room with an agitated mind, it has an impact on the people there. If they are not very secure themselves, they will become even more agitated by the sight of someone hurrying about out of control. Suppose the family is trying to get breakfast when in races the high school junior already late for school. She calls out to remind her mother to pick up her shoes from the repair shop on the way to the supermarket. She scrambles about trying to remember where she left her notebook. She spills some milk pouring it on her cereal, which she tries to eat standing up. In a few minutes the relaxed atmosphere in the room has dissipated, and everyone becomes edgy.

Happily, the opposite also holds true. When someone at peace and free from hurry enters a room, that person has a calming effect on everyone present. Such collectedness too is contagious. Until we learn to act in freedom, most of us will be temporarily calmed or agitated by those we are around.

Not only individuals, but even institutions can become insensitive to the needs of others under the pressure of speed. I have noticed that at some big boulevard intersections, there is not enough time for pedestrians to cross before the light changes. Disabled people just cannot make it and often give up trying. Older people must hold up their hands halfway across and appeal to the drivers not to run over them. Little children naturally need time to get across, but now they have to be dragged. What do we gain by all this? What harm is done if people get a few more seconds? Institutions like those that control traffic consist of individuals; let us urge them to reverse this trend. If we do not, the pedestrian signals may change. Where they now say STOP and WALK, they may soon say STOP and RUN — perhaps even FASTER! FASTER!

This encouragement to hurry has spread throughout our society. It has even touched reading. To get the maximum out of a good book or article, we need to go slowly and participate actively, asking questions of what we read and pondering the assertions. Now consider the advertisements for reading courses that appear even in respected newspapers and magazines. They claim they can teach you to read ten books in the time it used to take you to read one. But what kind of reading will it be? A wit said that after taking one of those courses, he read *War and Peace* in less than an hour and came away knowing it was about the Russians. Isn't it much better to read one worthwhile book with concentration, reflect on it, and assimilate it?

"HURRY SICKNESS"

Speed begets many physical disorders, often simply from stress. Digestive, breathing, and nervous problems may be cured when the pace of life slows down.

We may think stress strikes only at hard-driving professionals, but people in all occupations – bus drivers, police officers, teachers, construction workers, athletes – can fall victim. Doctors and therapists alleviate the symptoms, as indeed they should. But something more is called for, and that is a complete and permanent change in the patterns of living.

Often, physical problems constitute a clear call from the physical system that something in our daily life is destroying it. Pain, disease, loss of optimum health are meant by beneficent nature to be signals, very much like the signs on freeway ramps: "Stop! You are going the wrong way!" What clearer warning could we want? If we fail to heed this plain language, whom can we blame but ourselves? Unfortunately, we often refuse to accept this responsibility and cry out when diseases come, "Why me?"

In their classic research on Type A behavior, two brilliant San Francisco specialists, Drs. Meyer Friedman and Ray H. Rosenman, claimed there exists a particular kind of personality that is prone to heart attacks. Heart disease has long been linked to certain physical risk factors like hypertension, high cholesterol levels in the blood, smoking, and lack of exercise. But these doctors' research, first published in their book *Type A Behavior and Your Heart,* located the culprit in the lifestyle itself and the ways of thinking that produce it. Decades of research since then leave the Type A hypothesis controversial, but I think there can be no doubt that the syndrome these physicians identified is stressful in the extreme.

"Diet and cigarettes are the bullets," the doctors wrote, "but behavior is the gun." They believed that a primary cause of coronary artery and heart disease is a complex of emotional reactions "that can be observed in any person who is aggressively involved in a chronic, incessant struggle to achieve more and more in less and less time, and if required to do so, against the opposing efforts of other things or other persons."

In other words, one of the most distinctive features of such a personality is hurry. The hurried person, aggressively seeking satisfaction and profit, buys a heart attack. Imagine people waiting on the sidewalk for a department store to open during one of those gigantic, once-in-a-lifetime, all-must-go clearances. All kinds of people gather, shoving to get in. Then the doors open — the poor employee who opens them gets mashed up against the wall — and everybody runs in, yelling, "Where are the heart attacks?"

Characteristically, such people move, walk, and eat rapidly — and, I would add, think rapidly too. They become frustrated, even angry, if a car or person ahead of them goes too slowly. They cannot bear to watch someone take more time with a job than they would, even if the job is being done well. Waiting — at a restaurant, for the bank teller, in a checkout queue at the supermarket – is slow torture. Even to wait their turn in conversation can be excruciating, and when the person they are talking to is at a loss for words, they often rush in to finish the sentence themselves. After reading the list, many of us must be wondering how it happened that we were chosen as a model.

The hurried and harried person frequently tries to do two things at once. When you stop him at work to ask a question, he thinks about what he intends to do next. If you pause a little to choose your words, something pleasant and persuasive, he immediately fills the gap with his own, blunt and to the point. You always feel that he wants to get the conversation over with as soon as possible. When he swims – to relax, he maintains – his mind is on his personal and professional problems. Perhaps he has even arranged for phone calls to come to him at the poolside. While he shaves in the morning, he tries to eat breakfast, if he bothers with it at all. While running to catch the departing bus, he stuffs his papers into his briefcase. When he drives, he must hear the latest news, no matter how heavy the traffic. I am reminded of Thoreau's observation that most of us cannot lie down for a half-hour nap without asking when we wake up, "What's new? How has the world fared without me?"

THE COMPETITIVE DRIVE

The competitive drive exhibited in Type A individuals is often praised as a positive quality – the way to "get ahead." Yet any work undertaken in this spirit leads to impaired health and benefits no one.

Often in the classified section of the newspaper you will find advertisements that read, "Salesman wanted – must be aggressive." In other words, that person must be ready to force people to buy things they don't want or need. All of the ingenuity of the salesman, and it may be considerable, goes not to the task of serving people but is pitted against their will and judgment so that desires for superfluous things and services can be roused in them. "Aggressive" surely seems an accurate description. But while such techniques may improve sales, we should remember that in this case the salesman really buys as he sells, and he constantly sends in his orders for a long list of destructive physical and emotional ailments. His aggression is directed against himself as well as against his customers.

This competitive drive is not confined to making money or acquiring power either. It crops up in amateur games and sports intended chiefly for recreation. Winning, not enjoyment, becomes the goal, and misguided adults inflict this attitude on youngsters playing in baseball and football leagues.

Some people pursue a hobby with the same frantic intensity; they simply have to have more imported beer cans than anyone else in town. "Hurry sickness" afflicts not only people with important responsibilities or positions; competitive enthusiasm is all too often spent on trivia.

Even if the body of the hurried person manages to escape a heart attack or some other major disease, it becomes exhausted much earlier than need be. I am convinced that many of the problems we now associate with old age are completely avoidable. Most of us accept unquestioningly that at some point in the future we will grow senile, that we will fall in the bathtub, walk with a cane, or live entirely in the past. It is just a matter of time, we think, before we will be alone and helpless or an unwanted burden on others. I assure you that this does not have to happen, and one thing we can do right now is take steps to avoid hurry, which saps the body's vigor. When we rush about, our vitality ebbs rapidly; when we act calmly, we glow with strength and beauty even in the evening of life. My grandmother, for example, was vibrantly alive until the day she shed her body at an advanced age.

HOW CAN WE SLOW DOWN?

If we want freedom of action, good relations with others, health and vitality, calmness of mind, and the ability to grow, we have to learn to slow down. We simply cannot afford to pay the price of hurry, however attractive the packaging. The price is our very life. Again the profound words of Thoreau come to mind: "I have no time to be in a hurry."

But it is not enough just to say this or to put a sticker on our bumper: "You are following a slowpoke." We are dealing with a deeply imprinted pattern of behavior and long-standing habits. We need to have a strategy, take practical steps, and be prepared for a long struggle, though the benefits will accumulate as soon as we begin. It is we who must assume responsibility for changing these habits . . . for learning to slow down.

One practical step is to get up early in the morning. If you don't do that, how will it be possible for you to avoid hurry? Naturally, a certain number of things have to be done before you start work: you need to meditate, eat your breakfast, brush your teeth, and so forth. Obviously, if you wake up at eleven o'clock and then start a program of going slow, you won't be able to accomplish any work at all.

So get up as early as you can. In the country, the beauty of morning is unexcelled: the coolness, the special quality of the light, the dew on flowers and spiderwebs, the singing of the breeze, of the birds, of the whole earth. In the city too, things are at their best. There is relative quiet and the promise of new opportunities. Wordsworth found beauty even in the city in early morning:

> This City now doth, like a garment, wear
> The beauty of the morning; silent, bare,
> Ships, towers, domes, theatres, and temples lie
> Open unto the fields, and to the sky,
> All bright and glittering in the smokeless air.

When you rise, have your meditation at a fixed time, so that it will almost become a reflex. Just as many people feel famished at noon when it is time for their lunch, your mind will feel famished for meditation and will want thirty minutes to still itself. You may think that an extravagant claim, but why should the conditioning behind our habits always work against us? We can train ourselves to do automatically what benefits the body, mind, and spirit, just as now we too often compulsively do what harms them.

After meditation, if you have risen early, there will be time to go into the breakfast room, sit with your family or friends, say a few loving words, and go through your breakfast leisurely. In order to enjoy your food, or anything else for that matter, you have to learn to go slowly. But look at the number of people who eat and run. In fact, a restaurant near us has that name, "Eat and Run." I don't plan to go in. Running about is bad enough, but doing it after eating is simply asking for digestive trouble. I assume a lot of people do ask for it, though, because I see those little rolls of antacid pills sold like candy at counters everywhere.

I never heard of a restaurant in India called "Eat and Run," but modern life has left its imprint there in other ways. We have an interesting phenomenon called the "railway meal." I hope you never have to experience one. The railways serve meals right on the train when it pulls into a station, and you have about twenty minutes, or perhaps only fifteen, to eat. The man who brings the food just stands there hovering over you, concerned that the plate might go with you on the journey. He watches, he waits, and you know that the moment the bell rings, whether you have finished or not, he will snatch that plate away. People eat with arms flying to their faces, and after every mouthful they look at the time and quickly thrust some more food in their mouths. Consciousness is completely split between plate and watch. It doesn't make for a very enjoyable meal.

Often people forget, not because they have a poor memory, but because they rush. At campus, when the instructor asks for the papers, they have to say, "Oh! It's not here!" — adding, somewhat lamely, "I must have put it in the back of the other car." Actually, as they flutter around getting ready to leave, such people aren't really there. The madly dashing body bears some resemblance to the person you know, but the mind is not present. When you leave for work, for errands, for a trip, it is a good idea to slow down and spend a few moments checking through things mentally to make sure you are taking everything you need. Haven't you ridden with someone who, about two or three miles from home, suddenly slaps his forehead or groans because something was left behind? You must either turn around and go back — and the second departure always seems a bit less interesting — or phone to arrange a complicated plan for retrieving the missing object, or do without it. And all this because the person was "saving time" by hurrying to get out of the house.

How much better to arrange an early start! That way you won't have to arrive at the last moment and dash in with no time to be cordial to anyone. Why not be at your office, shop, or classroom ten minutes early and find out what others are doing? Chat with the people in the mail room; talk to the maintenance crew, who may have some interesting things to tell you.

Once, when I was on the Berkeley campus, I struck up a conversation with a man standing near me. I asked him what he did.

"Oh," he said, "I'm more important than the president of the university."

"Is that so?" I asked. "Who are you?"

"I'm the plumber," he said. "If the president doesn't come in, things are still okay for a while. But just let them try getting by without me."

Wherever you build personal relationships like this, people behave kindly. They will be understanding and give you their time if you will give them yours.

SLOWING DOWN AT WORK

At work, many people strive to squeeze in as many tasks as they conceivably can. Instead of concentrating on the essentials and doing what is required in a slow, thorough way, they hunt for the nonessentials and work on them first.

In India, we have an expression for this: "painting the bullock cart wheels." Your neighbor in the village, say, has some important things to do; his relatives are coming, and the house needs repairing. He says in a serious tone that he intends to do it, but first he wants to take just a little time to decorate the wheels of his bullock cart. The wheels on those carts are huge, and even an ordinary paint job on them takes a long while. If he starts to work in fancy designs, little triangles and curlicues in lots of different colors, the painting can drag on indefinitely. So he paints the wheels while the meaningful tasks go untouched. At the last minute, with a pointed reminder from his wife, he realizes that he can postpone no longer, and in a burst of agitation he rushes about to get the important things done. He usually doesn't succeed.

By postponing, you set the stage for a drama of crisis at a later date. When you can evade things no longer, you rush about frantically with your adrenalin pouring — body under stress, mind scattered — and barely squeeze by with a second-rate job. Or perhaps you miss the deadline altogether and have to accept penalties. I have a friend who lives near a post office that stays open until midnight. One April 15, when income taxes fell due, the postponers raced down there at about eleven-thirty at night to mail in their returns. Soon many, many cars were backed up, each with a driver anxiously waiting to get his or her envelope postmarked before the deadline. Finally a man saved everyone by coming out of the post office with a big cardboard box and walking down the street so people could throw their envelopes in it. But of course many others did not have their returns ready at all and had to give Uncle Sam a bonus.

At work, as elsewhere, we need to cultivate discrimination so we can decide what is important and then proceed to do it at a moderate pace. Hurried work and work done under pressure yield no joy, and that may be why so many of us don't even associate joy with work. We expect to find happiness after we leave for the day. But all truly creative people know that no sharp line lies between work and other activities. Work should challenge us – be difficult, if you will – but that is no reason for us not to find satisfaction in it. Quite the contrary.

But where hurry prevails, there can be no satisfaction for the doer. Hurry clouds judgment, and more and more a person thinks of pat solutions or shortcuts to save time and gives an uninspired, sloppy performance. He – or she – spills, shatters, rips, drenches, bursts, and burns things, not to mention the injuries, even serious ones, he inflicts on himself and others. Slowing down, on the other hand, is not inefficient. It means more efficiency. It means you will make fewer mistakes, have fewer accidents, and do a more creative job.

During the day – not only at work, but in the post office, restaurant, or bank – you can also combat the fast pace of others. Good spiritual manners require that you say to people who help you, "Take your time. I'm in no hurry." You can perform this service for those who serve you, and they will respond immediately. I remember standing in a queue in the Berkeley post office during the Christmas season amid much fuming and pawing of the tile floor. When I arrived at the window, I told the clerk I was not in a rush. She sighed, looked directly in my eyes, and thanked me. More than that, the people behind me heard me say it and became a little ashamed of their impatience; they too began to relax.

The patience we show at work, on errands, and at home is our insurance against all the distressing ailments brought about by hurry. Patience means good digestion; impatience means poor digestion, even gastrointestinal disorders. Patience means slow, deep breathing; impatience means poor lungs and irregular breathing. Patience means a slow, steady pulse; impatience means — well, find out for yourself by taking your pulse rate when you become angry. When you are patient, all the vital processes work smoothly. In the present context, patience means not hurrying when dealing with others and giving them as much of our time as they can profit from.

At the end of the workday, you might try to bring things to a close a little early so that you have time to clear off your bench or desk, put away tools or papers, and organize your materials for the following day. I understand that some executives never leave the office until their desks are cleared. We may not be able to go so far, but we can avoid the heaped-up, untidy work area that suggests a heaped-up, untidy mind.

EMERGENCIES

If we maintain a leisurely pace throughout the day, we have a better chance of arriving home safely. A large number of automobile accidents occur at twilight, and one reason seems obvious: we have been so drained by a day of hurry that our senses and mind are far less alert. In an emergency, those who are calm respond more quickly; they really observe what is happening in front of them. They grasp the connections between events better, see emergencies arising, whereas the vision of the hurried person is blurred.

The deliberate person acts promptly in the emergencies that demand it and acts in a more measured fashion at other times. In every case the response will be appropriate and freely chosen, not dictated by compulsion. Such a person can be contrasted with two extremes.

On the one hand, there are those who constantly hurry, hoping thereby to be more efficient. As we have seen, they fail to gain their objective. Something urgent, some kind of emergency, is always happening for them, and they are so overtaxed that they become incapable of responding to a genuine emergency when it arrives.

On the other hand, a few people cannot move quickly even when the occasion requires. Rather than take a good, brisk walk to put the muscles of the body to work, they dawdle along, often listening to their thoughts. They may not even sense when a real crisis has arisen, because they are absorbed in themselves. This is not what I mean by slowing down.

WHEN WORK IS OVER

At home, after returning from a day at work, most of us like to have an evening of recreation with family and friends. To enjoy such recreation, though, you need detachment from your work—the ability to drop it mentally at will. If you have been rushing all day, you will be so entangled and tense that you will not be able to let it go. While circumstances may require you to bring work home from time to time, it is something else again to leave the work there and bring the thought of it home, fretting over what has already happened and what may happen on the following day.

Think of a job as a kind of apparel. You walk in, slip into your occupational coat as, say, a librarian, well driller, city planner, or printer, and for eight hours you give yourself wholly to your job. But at the end of the day, you take off this coat and hang it on a hook; you don't stuff a sleeve into your back pocket or purse and drag the rest on the ground behind you all evening long and throughout the weekend. Working with concentration and then being able to drop your work at will is a skill that can be developed with practice. If you do not learn this kind of detachment, you will be burdened by work as Sinbad the Sailor was by the Old Man of the Sea, who straddled his neck, squeezing him with bony legs.

When you come home from a workday without hurry, once again to join your family and friends, you will be able to give freely of yourself. You may find as you walk in the door that some distressing situations have developed, especially if you have children. But since you have husbanded your vitality wisely, you will have sufficient patience to ease these domestic difficulties even though you have put in a full day's work.

Commonly people come home and say, "Don't bother me with it! I worked hard today." But though your employer may expect only eight hours from you, life is capricious and requires many more; we must be prepared to serve. Do you see how vulnerable we become if we insist on having everything just the way we want it when we return home? Every time things fall short of our desires, which may happen frequently, we will be frustrated and angry. In effect we are saying to life, "Please, please, let everything be just as I like it—lots of quiet, a refreshing drink, my slippers, the paper, and the reclining chair all ready. No difficulties, please . . . you know I can't take them."

I have been speaking of the person who leaves home for a day's work, but much of it applies equally to those who remain. There is the same need to set a leisurely pace and use discrimination in the performance of tasks, the same need to organize work and be able to drop it at will, the same need to be patient and considerate towards those around us, whether it be those who stay home with us, such as children and older folks, or those who return home, perhaps care-laden, from their day's activities.

In my native state of Kerala we have a beautiful tradition: every twilight the woman of the house lights a lamp, usually a brass one with the wick floating in coconut oil, and moves from one member of the family to another, displaying for all this symbol of their unity. Even without such a lamp every one of us can, through our love, be a radiant light in our home.

In the evening, when you have been reunited with those close to you, rushing and tension are completely out of place. Let us be relaxed and responsive to everyone. If the children want your attention, listen cheerfully, not with half a mind but fully; you will find it vivifying to see the world, your world, through a child's eyes. Some people rush so much that even when the day is over they miss this opportunity. Still hoping to get a lot more done, they easily become exasperated and shush their children or implore, "Can't you hurry?" What a blessing our children are not given to hurry! It is one of the things they can teach us. So we can ask for the day's news, find out what happened at school, ask them to repeat the big report they gave on the chief imports and exports of Paraguay. Not a very inspiring subject perhaps, but the love we feel in listening quite transforms it. When children belong in our lives in this way, they will not want to go out and do things which harm themselves and others.

People who claim they hurry in their work to gain more leisure time should not be taken seriously. In my observation, quite a number of them do not know how to enjoy their off hours. They have become addicted to excitement and excessive external stimulation. Some head for the new movie about demons or disasters certain to elevate their blood pressure and jolt them out of their humdrum existence. Others spend an evening wiping out their lucidity at some night spot featuring tall drinks and deafening music. Still others, having rushed all day, arrive late at a play or meeting and repeat, "Pardon me . . . pardon me . . ." as they distract the audience and step on their feet. And having blustered in, they probably won't remember where they parked the car — was it Polk Street or Jackson? Perhaps they quarrel about it, and since their speeded-up nerves have finally reached their limit, the whole day ends in an explosion.

FINAL SUGGESTIONS

How can we reverse these patterns of hurry and tension? The first thing, as I mentioned, is to rise early so you can set a relaxed pace for the day. Eat slowly at mealtime, sharing yourself generously with others. Arrive beforehand at your job and work on the essentials at a steady rate, not pushed by the clock or competition. Build friendly and loving relations with those at work and at home by practicing patience at every opportunity. Put things in order when you leave your job, and learn to detach yourself from your work at will. Cultivate discrimination in recreation so that you choose what really revitalizes and avoid what drains your time and energy.

The mantram is also particularly helpful in the case of hurry, because it gives the restless mind something to fasten on and gradually slows it down. Repeating the mantram on a brisk walk brings the words, breathing, footsteps, and mind into rhythmic harmony. An excellent way to take a short, refreshing break from work, it is also an aid in training yourself to drop your work at will. When you begin to feel yourself rushed, just stop a minute, repeat your mantram, and then be deliberately slow in whatever you are doing. On occasion you may have created a comic skit when you dropped something by rushing and, as you went to sweep it up, knocked something else over. Then you banged your shin, and so forth. The best course to follow at that time is to repeat the mantram a few times and recollect yourself so you can proceed at a measured pace.

Nor should we ever allow ourselves to be rushed by others. If the telephone rings while you are cooking dinner, find a convenient point to stop instead of immediately running to answer it and leaving the soup to boil over. We need not be intimidated by such things as telephones. After all, a phone call constitutes a request to talk to us, not an imperial command. If the message is important, the caller will stay on the line for a time or try again later.

I have another suggestion that may be of some value. When I recommend to someone that they slow down, they often raise a legitimate question: "There is so much that I have to do; how can I go through it slowly and get it all done?" I usually answer by referring to my own experience as a teacher in India. As chairman of the Department of English at a large university I had heavy responsibilities. But I wanted very much to train myself to do things slowly and without tension because I knew it would be a help on the spiritual path.

I began by making a list of all the activities I engaged in on the campus, the things that I was expected to do and the things that I liked doing. It turned out to be a long list. I said at the time what people tell me today: I simply cannot go slowly and take care of all these vital matters.

Then I remembered my spiritual teacher, my grandmother, who had great responsibilities in our extended family of over a hundred people and in our village. She always fulfilled those responsibilities splendidly, and I recalled that she had an unerring sense of what was central and what was peripheral. So, using her example, I started striking from my list activities not absolutely essential.

I was amazed at the number that could go. Those connected with colleges know the number of conferences, meetings, symposia, lectures, receptions, and so forth that it is generally assumed we have to attend. Often the gathering has very little to do with our chief duties. So I began to avoid those functions that I could not justify to myself. I thought at first that I would be censured when I no longer appeared at the monthly meeting of, say, the bicycle parking committee. But after several months of nonattendance, I noticed from the conversation of another member of the committee that he had not even noticed my absence. Putting aside my likes and dislikes, keeping my eye on what was necessary, using as much detachment as I could, I struck more and more from the list. Soon half of it was gone, and I found I had more time to give to what seemed likely to be of permanent value.

Reengineering our patterns in the ways I have mentioned will not be easy or painless. It will require persistent effort for a long time to reverse the patterns of hurry we have built up over the years. But the benefits are magnificent, and we begin to receive them the very first day we try to make these changes. From the beginning, we have embarked on a new course that will bring us abundant energy, better health, increased peace of mind, more harmonious relations with others, rich creativity in work and play, and a longer, happier span of life.

One-Pointed Attention

IF WE WANT to live in freedom, we must have complete mastery over our thoughts. For nearly all of us, it is just a euphemism to say we think our thoughts — actually our thoughts think us. They are in command, and we unwittingly serve them.

Let us imagine that you are a student and have just settled down to study for your finals. You have everything you need — sharpened pencils, textbooks, class notes, calculator, and a willing spirit — and you know you must really work at it because there is a lot of material to absorb. Turning to your economics text, you begin to read about the law of supply and demand... Suddenly, through a door on the far edge of your consciousness, a desire comes creeping in. It smacks its lips and whispers, "How about a pizza?" You have a serious purpose — these finals count — so you courageously reject the temptation and return to your reading. But the door is open now, so in rushes a memory of last week's rock concert, followed by a daydream about the swimming party next weekend. Again you return to your reading... or try to.

This question arises: if what you want to do is study, aren't these thoughts intruding without permission? Well, then, why don't you ask them to leave? We must face an unpleasant truth — they won't go. They know you're not the master here. And so there you sit, with half your mind on your studies, half on other things.

Suppose you find yourself troubled by some worry. It is a little thing, you would be the first to admit, but you can't shake it off. You go to a movie, thinking that will give you a fresh perspective, but the worry follows you and gnaws away at your consciousness like a mouse. Or perhaps you are sometimes possessed by song lyrics or bothered by a forgotten name; or you may play over and over again in your mind the tape recordings of pleasant and unpleasant moments, like that day at the ocean four years ago or the time Mary Sue snubbed you at the class reunion.

Or possibly more serious matters. A major error in judgment at work, carelessness that ended in injury for yourself or someone else, the memory of someone separated from you by estrangement or death, paralyzing fears and self-doubts, missed opportunities, debilitating addictions, envy and jealousy, a failure of will or some ethical lapse — how horribly any of these can haunt us; how they make us feel we have taken up residence in a sepulchre, far from the light and joy of day.

In all these common cases, the mind lacks an essential condition for clear thinking and smooth functioning: one-pointedness. In Sanskrit, this is called *ekagrata*. *Eka* means "one"; *agra* means "point" or "edge." "One-pointedness" is a very vivid expression, because it assumes quite accurately that the mind is an internal instrument which can either be brought to a single, powerful focus or left diffuse. Light, as you know, can be focused into an intense beam through the use of reflectors. But if holes and cracks lace the reflecting surface, the light will spill out in all directions. Similarly, when the mind is diffuse and many-pointed, it cannot be effective. The mental powers are divided up, and less remains available for the task at hand.

TRAINING THE MIND

Though our mind may be three-pointed or four-pointed or even a hundred-pointed now, we train it to be one-pointed in meditation. This remarkable discipline brings all the powers of the mind to an intense focus. We can say that it seals all our mental cracks and then sends the vital energy that was seeping out to the single point on which we have put our attention. As our meditation deepens, we shall discover that where we thought we had only a tiny, rather leaky light, we actually possess a tremendous beacon that can instantly illumine any problem.

In meditation we train the mind to be one-pointed by concentrating on a single subject – an inspirational passage. Whenever the mind wanders and becomes two-pointed, we give more attention to the passage – over and over and over again. It is certainly challenging work, but gradually the mind becomes disciplined, taking its proper place – not as the master of the house, but as a trusted, loyal servant whose capacities we respect.

Consider the practicality of having a disciplined mind. If you haven't trained your mind and you feel, for example, some resentment towards your neighbor, you may say, "Don't be resentful, my mind." But the mind answers superciliously, "To whom are you speaking?" When very angry, you add a "please," but the mind only responds, "You haven't taught me to obey you; why should I now?" And the mind has a case. If, however, you have learned to meditate and made your mind one-pointed, you have only to say, "No, my friend," when the mind gets unruly. There's the end of it. If the disturbance stems from a negative emotion like resentment, you will be able to draw your attention away and the distress will immediately be lessened. If it is actually a problem with a solution, you will be able to take some action later on to work it out.

In the Katha Upanishad we find a brilliant simile likening the mind to a chariot. Untrained horses can break away and run where they will, here and there, perhaps leading us to destruction, and what can we do about it? But trained horses – horse lovers know the delight of this – respond to even a light touch of the reins. Similarly, the mind well trained in meditation responds to a light, almost effortless touch. If the memory of a hostile act done to us by our partner tries to force its way in, we can eject it by turning our full attention to the many loving acts our partner has done in the past. Here we are refusing to be pulled about relentlessly by our thoughts – we are thinking them in full freedom. This is what the Buddha meant when he said, "There is nothing so obedient as a disciplined mind – and there is nothing so disobedient as an undisciplined mind."

THE BENEFITS OF ONE-POINTEDNESS

The one-pointed mind, once we have obtained it, gives us tremendous loyalty and steadfastness. Like grasshoppers jumping from one blade of grass to another, people who cannot concentrate move from thing to thing, activity to activity, person to person. On the other hand, those who can concentrate know how to remain still and absorbed. Such people are capable of sustained endeavor.

I'm reminded of a story about a great Indian musician, Ustad

Allauddin Khan. When Ravi Shankar, the sitarist, was a young man, he approached Khan Sahib for lessons, passionately promising to be a diligent pupil. The master turned his practiced eye upon Ravi and detected in his clothes and manner the signs of a dilettante. He said, "I don't teach butterflies." Fortunately, Ravi Shankar was able after many months — a test of his determination — to persuade the master to reconsider. But we can readily understand the teacher's reluctance to waste his precious gift on someone who might jump from interest to interest, dissipating all his creative energies.

People who cannot meet a challenge or turn in a good performance often suffer from a diffuse mind and not from any inherent incapacity. They may say, "I don't like this job," or "This isn't my kind of work," but actually they may just not know how to gather and use their powers. If they did, they might find that they do like the job, and that they can perform it competently. Whenever a task has seemed distasteful to me — and we all have to do such things at times — I have found that if I can give more attention to the work, it becomes more satisfying. We tend to think that unpleasantness is a quality of the job itself; more often it is a condition in the mind of the doer.

The same may be said for boredom. Few jobs are boring; we are bored chiefly because our minds are divided. Part of the mind performs the work at hand and part tries not to; part earns his wages while the other part sneaks out to do something else or tries to persuade the working half to quit. They fight over these contrary purposes, and this warfare consumes a tremendous amount of vital energy. We begin to feel fatigued, inattentive, restless, or bored; a grayness, a sort of pallor, covers everything.

How time-conscious we become! The hours creep, and the job, if it gets done at all, suffers. The result is a very ordinary, minimal performance, since hardly any energy remains with which to work; most of it goes to repair the sabotage by the unwilling worker.

When the mind is unified and fully employed at a task, we have abundant energy. The work, particularly if routine, is dispatched efficiently and easily, and we see it in the context of the whole into which it fits. We feel engaged; time does not press on us. Interestingly too, it seems to be a spiritual law that if we can concentrate fully on what we are doing, opportunities worthy of our concentration come along. This has been demonstrated over and over in the lives not only of mystics but of artists, scientists, and statesmen as well.

THE SECRET: ATTENTION

If we are to free ourselves from this tyrannical, many-pointed mind, we must develop some voluntary control over our attention. We must know how to put it where we want.

It is a sad fact that most people have little control over where their attention goes. That is why, for instance, billboards succeed so well. Advertisers know that we will not be able to pull our eyes away from those signs. Our associates may claim they are the masters of their faculties, but we have only to ride with them down a highway to see how easily their attention is snatched away and messages slipped into their consciousness. No matter how repugnant to our values and good sense, all those signs rush in, simply because we have no control over our attention.

Or watch people reading in libraries. When somebody walks

by – perhaps every few seconds – many people will lift their heads to watch. This is hardly a willed act; their attention simply runs about wherever it wishes. If we allowed our children to run about like that in a public building, we would earn looks of condemnation. But you can see attention running amuck everywhere.

Divided attention can lead to physical exhaustion too. Have you ever been completely worn out by a busy day of shopping, or by a visit to a museum in which you tried to cover everything from the Egyptian room to the French Impressionists? Being on your feet is part of it, of course, but allowing attention to shift rapidly from one sensory object to another depletes your vital energy and gives you very little in return. Probably you didn't give either the mummies or Monet the appreciation they deserve; about all you can say is that you have seen it all.

A famous specialist of the brain, Dr. Wilder Penfield, remarked that if he had his life to live over he would devote it to the study of human attention. For one thing, this faculty is intimately bound up with perception. Do you know the old proverb, "You are what you eat"? We can ring a variation on it by saying, "You see what you are." What you see in front of you is not precisely what is there, nor all of it, as any scientist will tell you. Vision depends on a complex internal process, one element of which is desire. What motivates us receives our attention, and whatever has our attention is what we see.

Ask four people what's happening on Main Street today. A businessman, just returning from a Rotary luncheon at the Livingstone Hotel, says, "Big crowd at Delfini's today. That guy sure knows how to move merchandise."

The elderly schoolteacher says, "Oh, something nice! Mr.

Delfini's nephew George is working in the store now."

A teenage girl tells you, "Delfini's is having this really neat sale."

And the teenage boy: "Wow, did you see those girls coming out of Delfini's?"

These people are simply reporting what they saw; their attention went automatically to the subject of their interest.

When through the practice of meditation we have gained a measure of control over our desires and learned to direct our attention where we want, the world will appear very different to us. More and more we will see things as they are, our vision unimpeded by compulsive attachments. Not only will we see the colors, textures, and shapes of things with greater clarity, but we will see the principles of harmony and order — or lamentably, in some cases, man's violations of these principles — in the objects and situations before us. So striking is the transformation in our ways of perceiving that Sri Ramakrishna, the nineteenth-century mystic of Bengal, speaks of growing "new eyes" and "new ears."

In a glorious outburst Thomas Traherne, the English mystic, tries to put into words the marvelous, ever-fresh appearance of the world to one whose eyes have been opened:

> The dust and stones of the street were as precious as gold ... The green trees, when I saw them first through one of the gates, transported and ravished me; their sweetness and unusual beauty made my heart to leap ... Boys and girls tumbling in the street, and playing, were moving jewels ... Eternity was manifested in the light of the day, and something infinite behind everything appeared.

Our attention, then, is a most precious faculty. It matters greatly what we do with it, because whatever we place our attention on, be it good or ill, is encouraged to flourish. If someone comes late to a public gathering and everybody turns to stare, they magnify the disturbance: they have given it their attention. If they can keep their attention fixed on the speaker, the clatter of the late-comer will be minimized. Similarly, if someone drops a plate or glass, how does it help to interrupt our business to stare? This is why I recommend that you not fight distractions in meditation. If you do, you give them your attention, your vital energy, and they swell up with it and are harder than ever to dislodge.

INVOLUNTARY ATTENTION

Occasionally we find people who have been gifted with one-pointed minds and have not had to undergo the strenuous sensory training necessary for most of us. Excellent — it saves a lot of effort — but there can be one potential drawback. Such a person's mind may fix itself so passionately on the subject of his interest that he cannot leave it even when necessary. As an educator, I am reminded of the professor whose entire concern is with ancient Sumerian or the late diary entries of Samuel Pepys. No matter where he goes, he carries that with him. This is certainly one-pointedness, but it's not volitional and can lead to poor social relations and minor mishaps.

Many stories are told about Albert Einstein, though I don't know if they can all be verified. Once, it is said, he received a check for a thousand dollars. A check like that makes a convenient bookmark, and that is how he used it until a librarian found it when the book came back. On another occasion, when someone asked whether he had had his lunch, Einstein replied, "Which way am I walking? If I'm going to my house, I haven't had it. If I'm coming, I have." And a passerby once saw him with a huge bulge in the shoulders of his coat; he had put it on without bothering to remove the hanger.

Einstein's contribution to science is so immense that this total absorption in his work seems more amusing to us than consequential. But for others it can take on a grimmer aspect. I remember reading about a man driving home from Carmel with his friends when he realized he had left his camera on the beach. He turned his car around and raced back at a terrific speed to retrieve it. His mind was fixed on that camera; he had to have it back. Tragically, he forfeited his life in an accident. So as we train ourselves to be one-pointed, we should strengthen our discrimination and will at the same time, so that we know where to put our attention and how to shift it when necessary.

ONE THING AT A TIME

If, as is the case for nearly all of us, our minds are indeed diffuse, how do we develop this valuable capacity of one-pointedness? The first step is the systematic practice of meditation, which is the perfect way to learn this skill. There is another valuable aid too: to refrain from doing more than one thing at a time, to abandon totally our habit of trying to perform several operations simultaneously.

I learned this emphatically when I was still a teenager. My uncle, my English teacher, had just introduced me to Washington Irving. I had read about Ichabod Crane frightened nearly to death by his own imagination and was well into the tale of

Rip Van Winkle one morning when it was time for breakfast. I brought my book and set it down beside the plate of rice cakes and coconut chutney. Chewing absentmindedly on the rice cakes, I read about poor Rip's reception by the village children when he returns after that long snooze. My grandmother, who had made the rice cakes with great love, just walked up quietly and took my plate of food away. I had not been aware of the taste, and for a few moments – I was really absorbed – I must have kept on lifting an empty hand to my mouth, because I heard her say, "You haven't got anything in your hand." I looked down for the plate . . . it was gone! Then she added, "This is poor reading. This is poor eating." I learned to put some distance between Washington Irving and rice cakes.

For a similar sight on this side of the world, visit Montgomery Street in the financial district of San Francisco. The favorite lunch of these financiers and would-be tycoons is not a Caesar salad or a club sandwich but a big serving of the *Wall Street Journal*. They may have some food on their plates, but all their attention is on the stock quotations, and that is what really goes in. You can see the same thing – different newspapers, of course – at soda fountains, truck stops, and coffeehouses.

Perhaps you know people who try to split their attention by reading books or newspapers even when they eat with their family or friends. It seems an inconsiderate thing to do, because it shuts other people out. In fact, I've seen a few who deliberately lift their newspapers up like a big shield which they hide behind so they won't have to see or be seen, talk or be talked to. But wouldn't those who love you rather look at your countenance – doleful as it may be some mornings – than at a full-page advertisement about saving seventy-three dollars by flying to Minneapolis on an after-midnight flight?

ONE-POINTEDNESS AND LEARNING

Take a walk through any college cafeteria and you will find students engaged in several activities at once. There may be one reading a textbook, having a cup of coffee, listening to music, and looking up every few minutes to see who is passing by – all at the same time. That is not one student; that is four quarter-students. All the powers of the mind have been divided up, and nothing is done with true absorption or true relish. I even saw a kind of circus feat on one occasion. A young fellow had a cigarette dangling from his lips – barely – while he sipped from his coffee cup!

Some students buy big bags of potato chips or nuts to snack on while they study in their rooms. Read a sentence or two, nibble. Read a sentence or two, nibble. Then, having interrupted the flow of logic in the text, they have to keep going back and rereading. Great progress is made in emptying the potato chip bag, but not much progress in mastering the subject. I have to confess that I have even seen teachers divide their attention in this way by bringing a pile of student papers to the conference room and setting about to correct them while a meeting was going on. Some, too, play radios in their offices while they read, when they should be illustrating for their students the ways of a dedicated teacher.

Anyone who deliberately divides his attention will find it more difficult to achieve mastery. Isn't it obvious that learning requires concentration? The really bright student understands this naturally. When he sits down to read and drink a cup of coffee at the same time, the coffee gets cold. If he has a cigarette in the ashtray it smokes away untouched — the best thing that could happen to it. If music is playing, he won't hear it. Such students stay completely concentrated and unaware of their surroundings. If you touch them or call them, they may not even know it.

You may remember Larry, the young American hero of Somerset Maugham's fine novel *The Razor's Edge.* The narrator tells us that when he entered the club library one morning, he saw Larry seated and reading with complete attention. When he left, probably in the late afternoon, Larry was still there, deeply absorbed, not having even changed his posture. Here, evidently, is someone with an unusual bent of mind, someone destined to excel in whatever activity he takes up. Later on, we find that nothing less than a spiritual awakening will satisfy Larry, and he begins his search with impressive singleness of purpose.

ONE-POINTEDNESS AND ENJOYMENT

Any person who has a great love for an art will scrupulously avoid splitting his concentration by doing two things at once. Take the lover of music. In a matter like this, you don't go by what people say — most people will claim to be devotees of music — but you watch them. True lovers of music will instinctively close their eyes when they are listening because they don't want any of their consciousness to be diverted. If you sit in a concert continually glancing around, your awareness is scattered; if I may say so, you're not only listening to the music, you're watching a movie too.

On the other hand, I've gone into bookstores and reading rooms and heard music being played. In such places there should be complete silence. Respect for the book we are reading demands it; even respect for the music demands it. The theory behind the use of music in such places is that it relaxes people. Music may relax people, but not when they're reading. The Buddha summed this up in his usual down-to-earth way when he said, "When you are walking, walk. When you are standing, stand. When you are sitting, sit. Don't wobble."

Some time ago I went to see the Royal Shakespeare Company stage *Romeo and Juliet.* The uncle of mine that I mentioned earlier introduced this play to me in my high school years, and one of the last communications I sent him before he shed his body was a program from this performance, with my thanks for passing on to me his great love of Shakespeare. The play began; I was completely concentrated. Fine actors and actresses all, and I responded very much to their delivery and to the beauty of the language and action.

Then came the famous balcony scene that touches everybody. No matter how blasé or hard-boiled you are, that scene will take you back to the bittersweet days when you were capable of such feelings. Juliet came onto the balcony; Romeo stood below, breathless with expectation. "But soft! What light through yonder window breaks? It is the east, and Juliet is the sun." The theater fell perfectly still.

Then I heard the words, "Where is the candy, please?" I know Shakespeare rather well, but — "Where is the candy, please?" I thought my memory must be slipping or that they played a different text than the one I'm used to. Perhaps Juliet wants to test Romeo's love... he should have brought candy if he wished to woo her.

Then I heard it repeated with more urgency, "Quick, where's the candy?" What a strange thing to be on Juliet's mind! Suddenly

I thought I detected a California accent — and sure enough, two high school girls seated next to me were having this competitive exchange with Romeo and Juliet. My grandmother's assessment applies here: these girls hadn't learned how to appreciate Shakespeare or how to enjoy candy.

Lovers of God possess intense concentration, as the biographies of the saints and sages show. In prayer, in adoration, in deep meditation, their attention rivets itself so completely onto the Beloved that nothing can tear it away. Even a suggestion of the divine — the holy name, an altar or relic, the sight of someone standing in a posture associated with an incarnation of God — may draw them into a higher state of consciousness. Occasionally this can be somewhat inconvenient, and it is said that one Italian mystic used to hide a little joke book in the sacristy so that when he said mass he could keep one foot on mundane ground and be sure to get the words out.

We read, too, that Sri Ramakrishna once went to see a religious drama produced by his disciple Girish Ghosh. He was very fond of Girish and of the play, so he sat right up front. The curtain went up, and a character started singing the praises of the Lord. Sri Ramakrishna immediately began to enter the supreme state of consciousness. The stage faded; the actors and actresses faded. As only a great mystic can, he uttered a protest: "I come here, Lord, to see a play staged by my disciple, and you send me into ecstasy. I won't let it happen!" And he started saying over and over, "Money…money…money," so as to keep some awareness of the temporal world.

Most of us obviously have the opposite problem: too little concentration. But we can learn to magnify our concentration by assiduously practicing this discipline of doing only one thing at a time. When you study, give yourself entirely to your books. When you go to a movie, concentrate completely on that; don't eat popcorn or talk to people. When you listen to music, do that and that alone. You will get more out of these activities, and your meditation will prosper.

I believe it a disservice to mix extraneous matters into our jobs too – a disservice to ourselves, to our employers, and to the work. The only way to draw out our deeper resources is to use fully what is presently available to us. Snacking, reading magazines, listening to music, gossiping, solving crossword puzzles, or making astrology charts at work divides and enervates our mental powers. Our conditioning alone leads us to believe that a divided mind is efficient. If we can unify our mind, we will see for ourselves that concentration breeds efficiency while division brings inefficiency, error, and tension.

ONE-POINTEDNESS AND SAFETY

Whatever the work, one-pointed attention averts mistakes and costly accidents. When you use powerful tools or dangerous instruments in the kitchen or shop, to provide an absolute measure of safety you should be totally concentrated on the task. I use the word "absolute" deliberately, and in the matter of safety I think we should strive for nothing less. It is not enough if we can say "This seems fairly safe" or "I think I can do that." We need a higher standard where the physical security of our body and the bodies of others is concerned.

What a pity to reduce safety by pointless distractions, such as blaring radios and irrelevant conversation. When you are in the kitchen, for example, cutting vegetables with an exceedingly sharp knife, is that a time to discuss who is going to win this year's Oscars? If you must discuss the Best Picture of the Year, put your knife down, get the other person's full attention, and then cast your vote.

Similarly, when operating a high-powered machine like a power saw or a Rototiller, you should not let your attention waver from the machine even for an instant. If someone enters the work area to talk to you, let him wait until you have finished that particular phase of the operation and can either shut the machine down or remove your hands and body from the hazardous zone. I hope you will see that this is actually good manners, and that it would be bad manners to whirl around suddenly and present someone an injured hand.

We can also further the one-pointedness of those operating machines by using caution in approaching them. It threatens their safety to rush into the work area or to shout near them or touch them. If it is essential that you talk with them, I suggest you try to edge slowly into their field of vision and wait until they are free. Anything that causes them to jump or lose their concentration can produce an accident.

I have noticed too that people go in for all kinds of talk while driving: political debates, quarrels, complex plans, jokes, anecdotes, even games. The driver should drive; the others can silently repeat the mantram. It's not just conversation; phones, music, radio programs, and even movies are common companions on the road. What a lot of distraction for the driver! Think of the serious consequences of it. Wouldn't you grieve if you seriously injured someone and knew that just an extra bit of vigilance might have made the difference? Simple reason demands that we recognize what we are doing: when we hurl our fragile bodies encased in several thousand pounds of steel down the highway at more than fifty miles per hour while others — who may be emotionally upset or very tired or even intoxicated — are coming at us at similar speeds, isn't it obvious that every bit of available attention should be used to avoid collisions? Anything less than full attention is simply irresponsible; it doesn't matter if we have managed to get away with it for any number of years.

It is incumbent on us not only to practice one-pointedness ourselves when we drive, but to help others to do it too. If you are a passenger, don't distract the driver. It may be true that the unhappy fellow has never seen a purple cow, and lo, one is grazing by the road — but then, if in the interest of reality I may be a bit grim, he may never have seen the inside of a hospital emergency room either, and it is far better to see neither sight than both.

PASSING ONE-POINTEDNESS TO OTHERS

Often we can gracefully remind people of this principle of one-pointedness. If someone talks to you while doing something else, you can say, "I'll wait until you are finished." If they are performing several tasks at once, you can say, "You seem to have your hands full; may I help?" Even a little playfulness might be appropriate. When you go to a film, you can gently reprove your friends with the old line, "I can't hear what you're saying for the noise they're making on the screen." Above all, our own example will instruct others.

Dentists, naturally enough, try to entertain us by chatting while they work. I had a very friendly dentist who wanted to reduce my awareness of the pain. I appreciated that, but I told him straight out that to show his affection for me he should attend to my teeth. I'd take care of the pain if he'd take care of my molars. He liked being free from the obligation of dental gossip.

Have you noticed how easily people become distracted when they are conversing? Their eyes roam about to their shoes, or the clouds, or passersby. Their hands flick about, picking imagined lint off their sleeves or drawing streaks on their moist coffee mugs. Their minds work up what they're going to say next, or, worse yet, pass over a number of irrelevant topics. When you listen to someone, listen with complete attention. In the Zen tradition the meditation teacher tells students, "Listen to me with all your ears, and don't take your eyes off me." Good advice. If your boyfriend begins telling you about the last chapter of his Great American Novel, as yet unwritten — keep both eyes on him so firmly that even if a peacock struts into the room fanning his tail, you won't notice. And when you admire the plumes of a peacock, give them all your attention, to the degree that you don't even hear the words of your would-be Melville.

Since children are less developed intellectually, we sometimes give them only a portion of our attention, believing that will satisfy their needs. We read a few paragraphs about the Middle East in a news magazine and then look up to say, "Oh, you're building a castle. That's nice." Then we jump back around the globe. The divided mind becomes a model for them, and we can be sure it registers on some level.

It also underestimates the capacities of children. When they play, they are not just passing time but learning, and we can help by giving discreet assistance when needed. If we have not been alert to their progress, we will err by failing to step in at the timely moment—or, worse, by interfering at the wrong moment. Children require a certain context for growth, and that includes, whenever possible, the presence of a loving adult fully alive to the situation and not one who has been pressed into custodial care.

We need to respect the child's one-pointedness. Even in infants, though the span may be very short, attention can be intense. Preschoolers are capable of remarkable concentration. I have read that a child in nursery school, having discovered a new operation with blocks, will perform it again and again as many as fifty times in total absorption. The table on which the blocks are resting and the chair with the child in it can even be moved across the room without disturbing this involvement.

CONCENTRATION IS CONSECRATION

Developing a one-pointed mind as suggested here will enrich your life moment by moment. You will find that your senses are keener, your emotions more stable, your intellect more lucid, your sensitivity to the needs of others heightened. Whatever you do, you will be there more fully. Entering a home, you won't slam the door because you will be there to hear it. You won't so easily trip or spill things or bump into people because you will be aware of your movements. You won't forget things, because now your mind is engaged. You won't become mentally fatigued, for you are conserving your powers. You will not be fickle or vacillating because you will have healed the mind of its divisions. And perhaps most precious of all, you will not ignore the distress or joy of others, because in looking into their eyes you will be looking truly into their hearts.

Achieving this precious — I might say wondrous — skill of one-pointedness will also greatly facilitate meditation and speed our progress on the spiritual path. Meditation is concentration, and concentration becomes, finally, consecration. As our absorption grows, we shall come to see that possessions, evanescent pleasures, fame, and all the power in the world can never satisfy us, but only that which is full of love and wisdom, that which does not pass. When we let our minds become scattered, we are but leaves on the surface of the lake of life, far from the infinite reality. When we unify our minds, we plunge deeper and deeper into that reality and move ever closer to the Lord.

Training the Senses

EVERYBODY, I THINK, values excellence. When the great masters in any field appear, we catch fire. I have always been interested in sports, and I still enjoy watching the Olympics or championship tennis on television; I am intrigued by the way the top athletes have trained their bodies, judgment, and endurance. Those excellent swimmers in their middle teens, those gymnasts who surpass circus performers, must have begun at a very early age. How much dedicated effort all this must take! It is hard not to admire the discipline and enthusiasm behind any performance that captures a gold medal.

Just as the body can be trained for virtuoso skills in the pool or on the uneven bars, so our senses can be trained, immensely benefiting ourselves and those around us. Then the senses become our trusted servants. But when they are untrained, as we shall see, they become the most oppressive masters.

Saint Francis of Assisi put the matter well. He used to speak of "Sister Moon" or "Brother Wolf" as though they were close relatives, which indeed they are; and with the detachment of a great mystic, he spoke that way about his body and senses too. "This is Brother Donkey," he would say, "and I'll take good care of him. I'll wash him, feed him, and give him rest. But I'm going to ride on him; he's not going to ride on me." Imagine walking along a country road in Italy when over a rise comes a peasant bent nearly to the ground by the donkey on his back. A ludicrous picture! But isn't that what we do when we let our senses and body take charge and issue all the orders? Believe me, they don't make kind masters; they are very demanding, very hard-riding. Through training the senses, we climb out from under them and regain our proper role as their master.

To put it another way, our senses are like puppies. If you have had a pup, you will recall how they seize a slipper and growl and tear at it until it's shredded. We expect that of puppies, but we don't want the dog acting that way when he grows up. To make a good companion of him requires training; fortunately, he loves to learn. Similarly, the senses can be the best of friends if they receive some training. But if we let them run loose without any training, they will simply turn against us.

HOW TO BEGIN

We begin the training of the senses by denying them things that injure the body. We wouldn't drive into a service station and ask the attendant to fill our gas tank with thirty-weight oil; the car wouldn't run. To operate a machine we have to use a particular type of lubricant, fuel, coolant, or whatever, and we do. But regarding our own bodies, we are not so careful. We put in all kinds of things that nutritionists — and plain common sense — tell us impair the body's smooth functioning, mainly because they taste pleasant. We haven't yet learned that the body's needs should determine what we eat, not the appeal of the senses.

As your awareness grows, it will hurt you to watch people let their senses drive them into harmful habits of living. When you see somebody smoke, you will understand the discomfort of those lungs. You will feel yourself in those air sacs, dreading the inrush of tobacco-laden air. Overeating will distress you too; you will hear the poor stomach crying out in its own language, "Please, please, don't stuff anything more into me! It hurts so." Whenever you see people damaging their bodies like this, you will be all the more vigilant about what goes into your own mouth. However tasty it used to seem, however aromatic or agreeable to the eye, food with no nutritional value will lose its appeal for you. And you will shun all those highly processed and synthetic foods which try to better nature: "balloon bread," cream without a cow, "instant breakfast," spray-can cheese.

Children especially are vulnerable to the appeal of the senses. We all know how television prompts a howl for breakfast cereals with little or no food value, simply because it tastes "neat" and comes in three different colors. Children below the age of judgment are urged to eat cereals consisting of as much as forty-five percent sugar, when they need solid nutrients for energy and growth. And all this so people can make some money! Worse yet, we go along with it by letting children watch these shows and giving in to their demands to eat what Booba the Bear eats — his Tooty-Fruity All-Jam Breakfast Triangles.

To wean children away from this, though, takes some time and energy on our part. We won't be able to say "Go watch TV" and hand them over to the set. We will have to be with them ourselves. And we can't say, "Honey, will you fix your own breakfast? You know where the Fruity Triangles are." It takes some effort to prepare a tasty, nutritious cereal of whole grains. We need time to prepare it, and time to sit down with the children so that all can enjoy it together.

Preparing healthful dishes also requires a rudimentary knowledge of nutrition. You needn't be an expert; it is enough to know the basic principles. But wherever you obtain your information, I would urge you to follow the findings of qualified experts rather than go in for fads.

AUTOMATIC EATING

The next step in training the sense of taste is to eat only when hungry. Food may lie close by, but no force compels us to eat it. Physicists have assured me that we can maintain a constant distance from food — or even increase our distance from it — just as easily as gravitate towards it. Most of us have been to dinner parties where the guests — after assuring the hostess they couldn't eat another mouthful — find themselves in the living room with bowls of mixed nuts and mints and cheese in strategic places. Soon all those bowls are emptied. No matter how often they are filled, empty they become. Someone says a few words and then pops in a mint. Another makes a smashing point about politics, then swirls a few peanuts in his fist and tosses them in. A third gets up to cross the room and makes a small detour by the Camembert on the way. We aren't really aware when we eat like this. Our attention is divided, and we eat compulsively rather than from hunger.

Automatic eating occurs too in front of the television set, or at a movie theater, nightclub, or sports event. The action catches us and the hand just keeps moving up and down, to and from the mouth, like an automated signboard of a cowboy endlessly waving "howdy" from a casino in Las Vegas. But we can learn to be more aware of what we are watching, and do one thing at a time. It will multiply our enjoyment immensely.

Eating has become so mechanical now that people eat and talk at the same time. I am not objecting to conversation passing across the table, which is certainly a part of the satisfaction of eating with friends or family. But it is quite another thing to try to talk about important or complicated matters with your mouth full of food. It just doesn't seem to be mannerly for me, say, to take a good bite of a corn muffin and then try to explain some point about meditation. Yet, I sometimes get the impression from the media that reporters and private detectives can't talk at all unless they have in hand a cup of coffee, a cigarette, or some sandwich sent up from a nearby delicatessen.

To train our sense of taste, we need to stop eating mechanically and become aware of what we eat. Eating only at mealtime helps, because we can focus our attention on the food more fully when we sit at the table. But give up snacks? What a terrifying prospect! The moment we feel a twinge of hunger — or even anticipate one — many of us head for the refrigerator or cookie jar. "No snacks means we'll get hungry. We'll have to wait all the way from lunch to dinner." What's wrong with that? It is good to be a little hungry. It enables us to relish food when we do eat. It lets our overworked stomach and digestive system complete their work before we give them more to process. And it helps in reducing total food intake, too.

ARTISTRY

If you do find that you have eaten more than you should at a particular meal — which is likely to happen to most of us occasionally — I have a simple suggestion for restoring the balance: skip the next meal. Instead of going about saying, "Why did I do it? Why did I do it?" and working yourself up to such a state that you head back to the refrigerator, just resolve to sail past the meal coming up. The mind loves to get entangled in all kinds of regrets, especially when it suspects you aren't really serious about changing your behavior. It says to itself, "I get to overeat, which I like; then I get to put on my black suit of woe and mope around for a while. I kind of like that, too!"

At a wedding or other special occasion, I enjoy being with my friends and sharing fully in the festivities. I don't want to be an Ebenezer Do-Good announcing in a funereal voice, "No pie for me; I'm on a rigorous program of sense-training." So if I know an elaborate meal is on the way, I go lightly on or even skip the meal that comes before. Then, at the feast, I participate in everything without overdoing it.

This requires a certain artistry. A while back one of my young friends made her entry into the world of the teens, and I joined in the celebration. Everything was carefully arranged for teenage tastes — "calories don't count." I sat down at the table and there was a big silver bowl of raspberry swirl ice cream looking up at me. But I didn't quail — I had prepared in advance by having a very light breakfast, and I ate the whole bowlful — and enjoyed it thoroughly.

But my taste buds were still smacking their lips. "Give us more!" That was the time to be firm. "That's it, boys," I said, and I gave all my attention to the friends seated around me. I can assure you, I found that much more satisfying than a second helping — and no need for "fast relief" from the pharmacy after I got home.

Gourmets claim that the true enjoyment of fine cuisine requires that you stop just when you would like to have a little bit more. In this way, the connoisseur maintains his interest. Everywhere, knowing how to stop short of satiety helps you to savor life and, more important, helps you to be free. At parties, instead of waiting far into the night until you are exhausted and the host doesn't know how to get rid of you, you can take your leave when there is still some life left. Even in letter writing, the same principle holds true. Haven't you received a letter of inordinate length and asked yourself why it couldn't have all been said in a couple of paragraphs? How much better for the recipient to say, "If only she had written a little more!"

VIGILANCE

We need to be vigilant in training the senses. For a long while we are so vulnerable that we can be caught at any time. The senses will be comfortably seated inside when some of their former pals — sense-objects — come to the door and call, "Can the senses come out and play?" At this point, of course, we can always say no. But if we are napping upstairs, the senses will jump up, look around, grin at each other, and rush right out.

We happen to pass by the pizza parlor, say, with the best intentions, just going to pick up a watch from the jeweler's. We have had our lunch; food is the farthest thing from our mind. But there is the big glass window with the fellow tossing powdery wheels of dough in the air, and we stop to watch. He opens the brick oven and slides out a hot pie with the cheese bubbling, topped with mushrooms...our favorite! Next thing we know, another mushroom pizza — ours — is bubbling in the oven, and we are trying to decide whether we want garlic dressing or bleu cheese on the salad. About halfway through we remember, rather guiltily, that we are trying to train our senses.

This kind of temptation may seem to lie everywhere. To the pizza parlor you may need to add the candy counter, the bakery, or the fast-food drive-in. But however many apply, you will surely gain mastery by working at it every day. There may be a few slips and falls, some close calls, but there will also be some rewarding victories. Just keep trying!

Because our habits are so deeply entrenched, we should not expect too much too fast. We have to assess just what we are capable of at any time. After all, we are trying to make our senses faithful servants, not abject slaves. We need to understand them and be firm but gentle: expect a little more from them than they have been used to, but not make unreasonable demands. We need to know when to issue strict orders, when to persuade and negotiate, and when to let them frisk a bit.

In the early days of your training it is helpful to have a few gambits you can play against your senses. They are simple fellows, really, and not that difficult to appease if you go about it the right way. If you crave candy, for example, you can offer your taste buds some nutritious substitute like raisins or fresh fruit. They will probably accept. Or when a sensory desire arises you might try saying, "Well, if you still want that in an hour, I'll give it to you." Very likely the desire will have subsided by that time, since it is the nature of desires to come and go.

The mantram can also be a ready ally in training the senses, especially when some negative emotion gets the better of us and we feel obliged to take it out on the refrigerator. Something goes wrong at work and we compulsively dispose of a few doughnuts or half of a pineapple cheesecake. It solves nothing; it only increases our mental agitation. Why not use the power of that negative emotion constructively? When we go out for a brisk walk repeating the mantram, we not only give our body a healthy workout, we transform negative emotions into their positive counterparts—anger into forgiveness, envy into sympathy, depression into good cheer.

Meditation, of course, is our most powerful tool for rechanneling our mind, for reconditioning ourselves. Sincere and regular practice can lead to complete transformation of the contents of consciousness. But even if we sit for meditation in the morning and then again in the evening, that will not of itself change our eating habits. We have to make wise choices during the day. Meditation gives us the freedom to make these choices, but we still have to make them. If we meditate for half an hour and then get up and head for the bakery, we wipe out the benefits of our meditation. But if we can use the power released in meditation to choose a wholesome breakfast instead, we are beginning to change ourselves. That is why I often speak of meditation and its allied disciplines: in this instance, meditation helps us train our senses, and training the senses draws on and deepens our meditation.

WE HAVE A CHOICE

All this requires personal responsibility. Many people, for example, gain weight and insist that nothing can be done. Such talk is not usually very persuasive, especially after a glance at their heaped-up plates. We can only go forward when we frankly admit that we have a weight problem because we eat too much, and we eat too much because we have not — as yet — trained ourselves to do otherwise.

I like to think of the contrast between two British writers, great favorites of mine when I was a professor of English in India: George Bernard Shaw and G. K. Chesterton. Both appeared often in the news, and even in India we heard a lot about their personal lives. What a difference between them! Shaw was a tall, thin man, not an ounce of extra weight on him. He took to vegetarianism when little was known about it in England, and the literary world feared that a promising writer would be cut off prematurely. The eminent physicians of London too warned him that his life would be shortened by his new way of eating. Of course, he went on to produce remarkable plays even in his eighties, and his friends naturally suggested that he go back to those physicians and show them how well he was doing. "I'd like to," he replied. "But unfortunately, none of them is around any more."

Chesterton, on the other hand, weighed three hundred pounds and hugely loved the pleasures of the table. You can imagine how they looked together when they met. Both had a marvelous sense of humor, and each enjoyed making rapier-sharp thrusts of wit at the other. Once, it is said, Chesterton cast an appraising eye on Shaw and said, "To look at you, GBS, one would think there was a famine in merry old England." And Shaw replied, "To look at you, GKC, one would know what caused it." So the question arises: do you want to look more like a GBS or more like a GKC? It is up to you. You can inflate yourself by eating wrong food in immoderate quantities, or you can have a trim, vital body by eating the right food in temperate quantities.

THE POWER OF CONDITIONING

The difficulty in resisting sensory desires comes from the force of conditioning working against us. When a river, for example, has gained momentum, how hard it is to stop it or even divert it! Most of our desires too flow like that, along deep channels cut in the mind through repetition. But just as a river can be rechanneled or dammed, well-established patterns of behavior can be changed. Naturally, the longer the channels have been there, the more work will be needed to remove them. But it can always be done, by drawing on the power released in meditation.

Most of the rigid likes and dislikes of our senses are picked up early in life. A mother gives her toddler a small dish of plain yogurt, and a neighbor, already conditioned, wrinkles up her nose with disgust and groans, "*Plain* yogurt?" Enough repetitions and the child's nervous system reacts automatically to the stimulus. He has been conditioned, and every time we are conditioned in this way, we lose a little of our freedom and our capacity to choose. That child has moved closer to the day when any food that is healthful but sour makes him wrinkle up his face and shove the plate away with a loud "No!"

Most of us have been through this. Usually, of course, we don't remember when, or where, or how we were conditioned. The person doing it probably did not know that he or she was teaching us how to react, putting limits on our consciousness. Actually, we begin to think that the unpleasantness lies in the food itself. We don't like the yogurt we have been served because it doesn't taste good, although next to us sits a lady happily savoring a big bowl of the very same thing, unflavored and unsweetened. It is the same yogurt; the conditioning is different.

I recently witnessed the enormous power of this conditioning in one of my young friends, who wants to be a football player. It happens too that he abhors zucchini, which I have found to be a rather harmless vegetable. So one day I said to him, "If the Lord came to you and said, 'I will make you the greatest football player in America if you eat zucchini every day,' what would your reply be?"

He was silent; I could see the battle going on in his consciousness. Finally he said, "I would tell him, 'No, Lord.'"

The power of likes can be just as strong. In my native state of Kerala, where cashews thrive, most of us are quite partial to them. I too shared this fondness. But when I left Kerala to teach at a university in central India, cashews more or less dropped out of my life.

Then, when I came to America, someone gave me a big can of cashews as a present. I opened it and was amazed at the response of my mind. All the old attraction came pouring in, and I could hear my mind say, "Ahh...at last! Cashews!"

But by this time I understood the ways of the mind, and I was training my senses. So I said, "Oh, you remember how good cashews taste, do you?"

The mind said, "Don't waste time talking...let's get to them!"

I replied, "I think you've forgotten again who's the boss around here. But I know you have a great fondness for these little nuts, and I'm a fair man, so I'll make a bargain with you. As soon as you stop clamoring for cashews in that insistent way of yours,

I'll give you some."

Then I placed the open can of cashews on the table beside me and turned to my academic work. For some time, the battle went on. I would be reading an incisive passage from Ralph Waldo Emerson, and suddenly I would feel something small and smooth touching my fingertips. Part of my mind — utterly unbeknown to me — had sent my hand over to the cashew can. "What's going on?" I asked gravely.

"Oh, nothing, nothing," the mind said. "We weren't going to *eat* any of them. We just wanted to see how they felt."

I didn't have to say anything more. My hand came back, and my mind scurried back to *The American Scholar* where it belonged.

At last, the mind gave up its tricks and subsided. I looked at the can of cashews and saw them for what they were — nuts, grown on trees in India where I used to live — and my mind did not move. "Good show," I said. "*Now* you may enjoy some." Those were the best cashews I have ever eaten in my life, because I ate them in freedom.

When you first learn to juggle with your likes and dislikes, there may be a lot of inner irritation. Some of the things you have chosen to eat taste so dreadful, and some you have chosen not to eat seem so luscious! But after a while, you will feel more than compensated by the marvelous juggling skill you are acquiring through your efforts. You may even begin, as the pulp magazines put it, to "amaze your friends and associates."

One young woman I know went into an ice cream parlor when she was beginning her sense training and asked the proprietor, "What's the worst flavor you have?"

"Licorice," the man said. "It's got to be licorice."

She ordered a bowlful and ate it all — and when she went to

pay, the man said with awe, "It's on the house."

After a while, you discover that your sense of enjoyment has been greatly multiplied. Freed from conditioning, you can now relish everything in perfect freedom — not only what you have always liked, but what you used to dislike too. You realize that taste lies in the mind, and the mind is yours to change.

SELECTING ENTERTAINMENT

So far we have been focusing on eating, but we do not eat with our mouths only. Eyes can eat. Ears can eat. And just as we exercise watchfulness about what we put in our mouths when we are training the senses, we have to be watchful about what passes through our other senses too.

A good play, for instance — one that explores character or expands our understanding, or even one that gives us some light entertainment — can be a wholesome meal for the mind. But a bad play is an all-you-can-eat smorgasbord; we stuff ourselves and often end up with a severe case of mental indigestion. And movies? I used to enjoy them, until I began to tire of seeing people throw off their clothes three or four times in an hour. But long ago, when I was training my senses, I discovered that even this can be turned into an opportunity.

Before a torrid scene came on, I recall, the whole theater would be fidgety. You could hear some talking and coughing, some candy wrapper and popcorn noises here and there. Then, suddenly, there would be complete quiet, complete concentration. Nobody would move, unless it was to the edge of the seat to get a closer view.

At this point, I began to do a very difficult thing: I closed my eyes. Or rather, I tried to close my eyes. I put my hands over them, but usually a chink would open up. After a while I managed to keep the lids closed, but the eyeballs still struggled and cried out, "This goes beyond the possible!" However, I persevered: if I was going to look at something, I wanted at least to have some say in the matter. I didn't want any of my responses to be automatic.

In this way, bit by bit, I gained mastery over my sense of sight. After that, I was free to use my eyes as I liked – and instead of watching the screen during such scenes, I began to look at the rest of the audience. Then I came to understand the nature of compulsion. What power! If only those people could have harnessed that concentration in meditation.

By such training, what once seemed a grand thrill now appears in its true perspective. As spiritual awareness grows, we begin to realize that this body itself is a kind of garment, the ultimate costume. It just is not possible to be really naked until we shed the body in death.

I remember when my nieces dressed up for a wedding and showed me their little white gloves. One said, "Uncle, you don't have on any gloves!"

I held out my hands and replied, "Oh, yes, I have – custom made, too. A perfect fit; you can't even see the seams."

When you have this realization, you lose interest in seeing people take off their shoes or shirt. You know they are still fully clothed, and the whole thing seems not wicked but rather boring. Today, when such scenes arrive on the screen, I often doze.

In the name of hard-hitting communication, the media increasingly also offer us debased language – a few shopworn vulgarities, hauled out to serve every occasion. Presumably they are supposed to shock us, but what I find shocking is that people will allow the full range of their expressiveness to be encapsulated in a few stale interjections. It may seem old-fashioned, but I would recommend standing guard over the gate of the mouth to ensure that only the right kind of words come out. It is another form of sense training. Vulgar speech, sarcasm, gossip, even pointless chatter, should all be denied exit visas.

The Sufis capture this idea in a splendid metaphor. They advise us to speak only after our words have managed to issue through three gates. At the first gate we ask ourselves, "Are these words true?" If so, let them pass on; if not, back they go.

At the second gate we ask, "Are they kind?" If we still feel we must speak out, we need to choose words that will be supportive and loving, not words that embarrass or wound another person.

At the final gate, we ask, "Are they necessary?" They may be true, even kind, but it doesn't follow that they have to be uttered; they must serve some meaningful purpose. Do they clarify the situation or help someone? Or do they strike a discordant or irrelevant note?

All of us understand what blows can do to someone, but we do not realize that words can create a more painful injury, one that can last for many years. Nor do we understand the terribly destructive impact words can have on the consciousness of the person who uses them.

THE POWER OF THOUGHTS

Even thoughts leave a powerful imprint on the mind. The Buddha says forcefully, "All that we are is the result of what we have thought." And on several occasions, Jesus pointed out that just thinking about an action can affect our consciousness almost as much as the actual performance.

All of us are appalled by the increase in violent crime across our land. We respond by buying more guns, training fiercer watch-dogs, installing stronger locks and higher fences. We have not yet recognized that we live in an increasingly violent physical world because we have chosen — largely through the media — to live in an increasingly violent mental one.

Every time we see a show or read a story filled with violence, our minds are being steeped in that, just as they would be if we saw real violence. More amazing, we voluntarily pay for this kind of violence, witness it, and make it real inside our mind. When we do this over and over, we become insensitive to it. Gradually violence becomes a possible solution to frustration, poverty, and injustice; we may even end up applauding it.

In being selective about what we take in from the media, we shield ourselves from so many banal concepts which turn us away from the permanent joy within our hearts. How often we have been shown the same tired ideas: to smoke and drink is the mark of sophistication, to drive at dizzying speeds is the mark of courage, to have a new partner every day is the mark of mascu-linity or femininity, to use violence is the mark of strength, to be uninvolved is the mark of freedom. No wonder the mystics say our world is upside down! To be secure everywhere is the mark of sophistication, to be unshakable is the mark of courage, to be permanently in love with every person is the mark of mascu-linity or femininity, to forgive is the mark of strength, to govern our senses and passions is the mark of freedom.

THE GOAL

When we stimulate the senses unduly, vitality flows out through them like water from a leaky pail, leaving us drained physically, emotionally, and spiritually. Those who indulge themselves in sense stimulation throughout their lives often end up exhausted, with an enfeebled will and little capacity to love others. But when we train the senses we conserve our vital energy, the very stuff of life. Patient and secure within, we do not have to look to externals for satisfaction. No matter what happens outside – whether events are for or against us, however people behave towards us, whether we get what pleases us or do not – we are in no way dependent. Then it is that we can give freely to others; then it is that we can love.

The implications of this are enormous. The historian Arnold Toynbee has characterized our civilization as sensate, lacking a spiritual foundation. A grave charge, but I think we have to accept its validity. And society is growing more and more sense-oriented, which means that people will be trying ever more desperately to cling to what is, by its very nature, transitory – the momentary pleasures of the eye, the ear, the taste buds, the body. This is not a matter of right and wrong, but a matter of logic. If you have within you, as all of us do, a need that can be filled only by what is permanent, how can you fill that need with what is fleeting – sometimes there, sometimes absent, never to be counted on? If you are on a sinking ship, you do not want a block of ice that will be gone before you reach the shore; you want a good, solid boat with a rudder that will steer you home.

By now it will be clear that training the senses means training the mind as well. If we could become detached observers of what happens in the mind when we see a piece of apple strudel or the current sex symbol in a film, we would find that a wave of desire has risen, agitating our mind as a wave agitates the surface of a lake. Where there are many strong desires, the mind is in constant turmoil. Huge waves lash and roil the surface, and we cannot see the bottom of the lake of the mind: our true Self. When we learn to train our senses and master our desires, fewer and fewer of these waves rise up. Gradually the mind becomes still, so that we can discover our real identity. Every major religion emphasizes this: to realize God, we must quiet the mind. As the Bible says, "Be still and know that I am God."

When the senses are trained, they will participate harmoniously in this supreme stilling of the mind. As we interact with people, as we work and play, we of course need to send our senses out a bit. But in deep meditation they will obediently return, as good servants should when the master or mistress — the soul — is entertaining a special guest — the Beloved. Saint Teresa of Avila beautifully expresses this goal, attainable by anyone who will undergo the training:

> You will at once feel your senses gather themselves. They seem like bees which return to the hive and then shut themselves up to work at the making of honey; and this will take place without effort or care on your part... At the first call of the will they come back more and more quickly. At last, after many and many exercises of this kind, God disposes them to a state of absolute repose and perfect contemplation.

Putting Others First

MY GRANDMOTHER WAS a remarkable woman. We come from a tradition that has been matriarchal for centuries, and within our large extended family — over a hundred people — Granny had weighty responsibilities. She liked to get up before dawn, long before the heat of the tropical sun became oppressive, and though I don't remember her doing anything just for herself, she would work throughout the day. Self-reliant, afraid of nothing, she stood steady as a pillar when a crisis arose — a death in the family, for instance, or a failure in the crops. In worship, in work, she set an example for everyone.

But Granny knew how to play too. She could throw off her years and join the children at their games — and not just the girls either; she played hard with the boys at tag and ball, and usually got the better of us. During a particular annual festival, she liked to stand up on the bamboo and palm swing we had fashioned in the courtyard, single out one of the strongest boys, and say, "Push me as high as you can!" And up, up she would go in prodigious arcs, wood groaning from the strain, while the women gasped and we boys stared in admiration below.

Granny possessed a great secret: she knew how to put others

first. If she bothered to think about her own needs, it was only after everyone else had been taken care of. I think especially of little things that mean so much to a child. On school days, she always prepared something special for my lunch – a favorite dish, a treat – and I would run all the way home to be with her. "Here comes the Malabar Express!" she would say. Then, though it wasn't her own lunch time, she would sit next to me and keep me company as I ate. One of the village priests called her "Big Mother" – I imagine because she nurtured and sustained us so well.

At one point, when I developed some illness or other, the local doctor prescribed a saltless diet for a year. Three hundred and sixty-five days without salt! I cannot convey to you what a sentence that was. In a tropical country where salt figures into almost every dish . . . well, my school friends said, "Why don't you just throw yourself into the river?"

The day after the order had been given, I came to breakfast with a long, long face. "What's the use?" I said, staring down at my plate. Everyone gave me a look of commiseration. But what could they do? They felt helpless.

But not Granny. Serving me, she said quietly, "I am going on a saltless diet for a year too." I don't think I have ever had a better breakfast.

I said Granny possessed a great secret, but that wasn't because she hid anything. The sad truth is that most people do not want this knowledge – chiefly, I think, because they fail to see the joy it brings, the sense of freedom.

One day I came home after school with something deeply disturbing on my mind: I had seen, for the first time, a child with elephantiasis. It is a terrifying disease, one that we are fortunately free of in this country. This little boy's legs had swollen badly. He walked only with great effort and of course he was unable to join in our games. I told my grandmother about him. "Granny, it must be awful for that boy to have elephantiasis and not to play."

Her face became very compassionate. She said, "Yes, everything in life will be hard for him." Then she added, "But only one in a million suffers from elephantiasis of the leg. There is a much more dreadful disease that can afflict every one of us if we don't guard ourselves against it all the time."

"What's that, Granny?"

"Elephantiasis of the ego."

The more I have pondered that remark down the years, the more perceptive it seems. Our swollen concern for ourselves, she was saying, constitutes the worst threat in life. And the teachings of every religion bear her out. Repeatedly we are told that ego or self-will, our drive to be separate from the wholeness of creation, is the source of all our suffering. It keeps us from accepting others, from sympathy and quick understanding. More than that, it alienates us from the supreme reality we call God. It alone prevents us from knowing that, as Meher Baba put it, "You and I are not 'we'; you and I are one."

Puffed up by our self-will, we look out at the world through the distorting medium of our likes and dislikes, hopes and fears, opinions and judgments. We want everyone to behave as we think they should – the right way. When, naturally enough, they not only behave their own way but expect us to do as they do, we get agitated. And what we see through this agitation makes up our everyday reality.

THE EGO

The word ego, as you may know, comes from the Latin for "I." Sanskrit too has a precise term for self-will: *ahamkara,* from *aham,* "I," and *kara,* "maker." Ahamkara is the force that continuously creates our sense of I-ness and its close companions "me," "my," and "mine." Independent of any situation, something deep within us, as persistent as our heartbeat, constantly renews our sense of separateness. Whether we are awake or asleep our ego goes on, though we are more conscious of it at some times than at others. Since it is always there, we think of it as our identity, and we protect it as a miser does his gold. Not only that, we expect others to treasure it too.

Management consultants advise their executive clients to establish priorities before they start to work. The ego creates priorities too. At the top of one of those legal-sized yellow pads it puts "To Be Taken Care Of." Below, on the first line, it writes "Me." There follows a list of all its requirements, which take up most of the page. At the bottom come the needs of those around. Oh, yes, if there are time and energy and resources left over, we will give them freely to others. But by and large, we must be served first.

Ironically, this drive for self-aggrandizement has never led to happiness and never will. We cannot always have what we want; it is childish to think so. No one has the power to regulate this changing world so that he or she can continuously sing, "Everything's going my way" — if we could do so, it would only stunt our growth. I have heard that even simple organisms placed in an ideal environment — controlled temperature, plenty of food, no stress of any kind — soon perish. Luckily, no one is likely to put us in such a situation.

"For those whom ego overcomes," the Buddha says, "sufferings spread like wild grass." You must have seen crabgrass or dandelions take over a lawn. In the countryside where I live, our fields have an even fiercer threat: thistles. The first spring only a few appear. You can walk through the grass without any trouble from them, and if you don't know their ways, you may not bother to remove them. After all, the flowers are a lovely color, and who doesn't like thistle honey?

But the next year, the "stickers" have spread. Big patches stand here and there, small clusters are everywhere; you cannot cross the field without feeling their sting. And after a year or two, the whole field becomes a tangle of tall, strong thistles; it is agony to walk through.

Similarly, the Buddha tells us, self-will inevitably leads to increasing frustration and pain. What a strange situation! We desire, naturally enough, to be happy. But if we put our personal happiness at the top of the list, we only succeed in making ourselves miserable.

"PERSONALITY"

When a villager in India wants a monkey for a pet, he cuts a small hole in a fresh coconut and sets it on the ground. A monkey — usually an immature one — sees it, swings down, squeezes a paw through the tiny opening, and grabs a big fistful of the juicy kernel. Then comes a surprise: the hole is too small; both paw and food cannot come out together. But the little monkey will not let go! It simply cannot pass by a delicacy; so it hops around pitifully with a coconut dangling from its arm until the villager walks up and claims his new pet.

So it is with us. The ego lures us; its promises are so appealing that we cannot let them go. But in the end self-will entraps us, and we lose our freedom. Worse, we have found ways in the modern world to heighten our distress. Take the contemporary cult of personality. Nearly everyone wants to be visibly unique, to be charismatic, to have a dazzling personality. "Have you met Mr. Wonderful? He's witty, talented, and so good-looking!" Madison Avenue stands ready as ever to help us fulfill these aspirations with products that proclaim, "Now you can be the you you have always wanted you to be" — if, of course, you rinse your hair with Lady Nature Herbal-Protein Concentrate or splash on Le Sauvage aftershave.

"Personality" happens to be a perfect word here. It too comes from Latin: *persona,* the term for the face masks worn in ancient Greek and Roman plays. Have you seen sketches of them? How stony they look, how rigidly fixed! All the fluidity, all the spontaneity of the human countenance was missing. Whether he wore the downturned mouth of the tragic mask or the grin of the comic, the actor was stuck with it throughout the play.

Our much-valued personalities are usually just like that — rigid and inflexible. We work up a particular concept of who we are and strive to live it whatever the circumstances. We think of ourselves as hard-boiled and commanding, and act harshly when we should be tender. Or we think of ourselves as kind-hearted and behave sentimentally when we should be firm.

Those old masks amplified the voice so it could be heard throughout a vast amphitheater. That was good; the Greek playwrights were worth listening to. Not long ago I was walking with some friends when along came a car with a public address system attached to the top. "Hello!" boomed a smug, disembodied voice. "I'll bet you're surprised to hear me talking to you!" Hundreds of watts of power and the fellow had nothing to say!

We may not actually carry around a public address system, but most of us want our personality to be widely known and admired. If people do not think of us — and think well of us — a good part of the time, something must be amiss, and we turn to a course, a book, a therapy, a health spa, or a different hairstyle.

This desire for attention not only leads us into affectations of dress, speech, and gesture; it also divides our consciousness. A small portion of our mind may be aware of the needs of others, but the larger portion is preoccupied with the effects we are creating. If the role does not fit, we will be self-conscious and ill at ease, never quite sure if we are going to be booed off the stage.

Surprisingly, when we stop trying to live up to an artificial image of ourselves, our real personality bursts forth — vivid, appealing, unique. Look at the lives of the great mystics — Francis of Assisi, Teresa of Avila, Sri Ramakrishna, Mahatma Gandhi. These are not drab figures stamped from the same mold; never has human personality been more dynamic, more spontaneous, more joyful, more strikingly individual. Saint Teresa, for example, underwent severe trials in setting up her order of Carmelites, but about her always hovered a wonderful playfulness. When the bell rang for recreation in the convent at Salamanca, the novices used to rush to block Teresa's way, gently tugging at her habit and cajoling her, "Mother?" "Dear Mother!" "Isn't Your Reverence staying with us?" She would laugh and yield, tarrying to compose some *coplas* which the whole convent sang, all clapping hands and dancing together.

Next to someone like this, for whom joy became a continuous presence, it is we whose lives must seem uniform and routine. No wonder Traherne says, "Till you can sing and rejoice and delight in God as misers do in gold and kings in sceptres, you never enjoy the world"!

LOVE

It is only by giving up this attempt to put ourselves first that we can find what we really want — peace of mind, lasting relationships, love. Do you remember the children's game "King of the Mountain" — scrambling up the sand pile, pulling and pushing each other to get on top? That may be all right when we are seven years old, but when we are twenty-seven — or fifty-seven? By the time we become adults, we should begin to think of leaving these scrambling games behind.

Eradicating self-will is the means by which we realize the supreme goal of the spiritual life. This is what all the great mystics have done, and done completely, through years of strenuous effort. True, if we set out to do it, we are going to find it difficult and uncomfortable for a long while. But what freedom we experience when that monstrous impediment we call the ego is finally removed! Says Saint Bernard of Clairvaux:

> Just as air flooded with the light of the sun is
> transformed into the same splendor of light, so
> that it appears not so much lighted up as to be
> light itself, so it will inevitably happen that every
> human affection will then, in some ineffable
> manner, melt away from self and be entirely

transfused... The substance indeed will remain, but in another form, another glory, and another power...

In this self-naughting lies the power of life itself, and through it we are born anew. This is what Jesus meant when he said, "If you want to find your life, you have to lose it." It is what Gandhi meant when he said, in response to the suggestion that he was without ambition: "Oh, no, I have the greatest ambition imaginable. I want to make myself zero."

What concrete steps can we take to bring this about? What can we do day by day?

When my grandmother told me about elephantiasis of the ego, I remember I asked her whether there was any cure for this malady. "Oh, yes," she said. "Love of God."

Love of God? Some may say it was natural that Granny would use those words, with her devotional Hindu background. You might even hear them among a few pious people in the West. But what can they possibly mean to us? If the materialistic bent of our culture has not banished such devotion, our intellectual training has. How can we conceivably have a fervent love of God in our times? It is a good question, and I think there is a practical answer to it.

First, we need to ask what we mean by "love." The term has been used so shamelessly in connection with all kinds of things — soft drinks, paper towels, garage door openers. And love between a man and a woman, we are told, means a muscular, tanned fellow running hand in hand through the surf with a stunning, billowy-haired girl, or couples sitting across glasses of wine at a little hideaway restaurant. From such imagery we draw our romantic notions of love.

But listen to Saint Paul, in his First Letter to the Corinthians:

> Love is patient; love is kind and envies no one. Love is never boastful, nor conceited, nor rude; never selfish, not quick to take offense. Love keeps no score of wrongs; does not gloat over others' sins, but delights in the truth. There is nothing love cannot face; there is no limit to its faith, its hope, and its endurance. Love will never come to an end.

That is a love worthy of us. That is a love powerful enough to dissolve our self-will.

When Jesus urged us to love God, he added also: "Thou shalt love thy neighbor as thyself." The two interconnect. The Lord is present in every one of us, and when we love those around us, we are loving him. The Hindu scriptures put it memorably:

> When a man loves his wife more than himself, he is loving the Lord in her. When a woman loves her husband more than herself, she is loving the Lord in him. When parents love their children more than themselves, they are loving the Lord in them.

EVERYONE CAN LEARN TO LOVE

I once spoke to a group of high school girls at a luncheon in Minneapolis. After my talk I answered questions, and the girl who presided asked, "You've used the word *love* many times. What does love mean to you?" I gave her the same answer: "When your boyfriend's welfare means more to you than your own, you are in love." This girl turned to the rest of the gathering and said candidly, "Well, I guess none of us has ever been in love."

I think that can be said for most people. But we can *learn* to be in love. The spiritual life is marvelously fair: it is open to everybody. No favoritism, no hereditary class. No matter where you start, you can learn everything you need to learn, provided you are prepared to work at it. So too of love. Any one of us may be very self-willed now, but why should we be depressed about it? We can begin the work of eradicating our self-will, and the easiest and most natural way is by putting the welfare of those around us first.

In a sense, it comes down to attention. When we are pre-occupied with ourselves — *our* thoughts, *our* desires, *our* preferences — we cannot help becoming insensitive to others' needs. We can pay attention only to so much, and all our attention rests on ourselves. When we turn away from ourselves, even if only a little, we begin to see what is really best for those we love.

Hugh, for instance, really looks forward to watching *The Wide World of Sports* every weekend. He has done it for years. "I've had a hard week," he says, puts up his stockinged feet on the ottoman, and leans back.

But what about his wife, Elaine? Was *her* week so easy? He might ask her what she would like to do. Go to the beach? Shop? Get the garden started? It might be painful to pry himself away, but if he loves her — and if he wants to grow — he will choose to read the scores in Monday's paper.

For Hugh it may be *The Wide World of Sports* that has to be forgone; for another it may be a shopping trip, a nap, a chance to make some extra money, a hobby, an unfinished painting. Whatever it is, giving it up, even temporarily, may hurt. Our preferences are sticky, like the adhesive on a bandage; there may be a wince when we tear them away. But it has to be done if we want to relate easily and lovingly with those around.

Any time we refrain from self-centered ways of acting, speaking and even thinking, we are putting others first. Anger, for example, is often nothing more than violated self-will. Hugh expected a bonus and didn't get it, so he sulks. Elaine wants their son Jack to stop tinkering with his car and spend more time on his schoolwork, but Jack has other ideas; both get resentful and quarrel. To be blunt, when we are crossed like this by people or events, we do our human equivalent of roaring, baring our fangs, and lashing out with claw, horn, tail, or hoof. The household can become quite a menagerie.

But anger is power, and Hugh, Elaine, and all the rest of us can learn to harness this power by putting each other first. Whatever the flavor of our anger — irritability, rage, stubbornness, belligerence, or sullen silence — it can all be transformed into compassion and understanding. Those we live with will certainly benefit from that, and so will we.

This does not mean that if someone we love tries to do something foolish or injurious, we should ignore it or connive at it by saying, "Whatever you want, dear." Putting others first does not at all entail making ourselves into a doormat. In fact, if we really love someone, we will find it necessary to speak out for that person's real and long-term interest — even to the point of loving, tender, but firm opposition.

Often the way we do this makes all the difference. If we are accusing or resentful we will seem entangled, judgmental, just the opposite of loving. Our words, our facial expressions, may betray a lack of respect: "I knew you couldn't stay on that diet, Hugh!"

Even with the best of conscious intentions, we may provoke a nasty clash. But if we can support the other person and express our disapproval tenderly, with respect, it will help him or her to see more clearly. When we have such a helpmate, my grandmother used to say, we do not need a mirror.

Lately I have run across best-selling books encouraging people to compete with each other, even with one's own husband or wife. Many couples, I hear, have taken this advice. Who brings home the most income? Who has the most promising career? I have even seen couples compete over their friends — or, tragically, for the love of their own children. But a man and woman brought into union are not adversaries. They are meant to complete each other, not to compete. Their union should dissolve separate boundaries — what is bad for one can never be good for the other.

PATIENCE

In my experience, love can be fairly well summed up in a single word: patience. Oh, I know it isn't thought to be a glamorous quality. I don't remember anyone writing a song about it. We can turn on the radio and hear songs about coral lips and pearly teeth, about candlelight and moonlight, about Paris and Rio ... nothing about patience. But you can have very ordinary lips and uneven teeth, live in Hoboken and never travel, and still have the most ardent love affair with your husband or wife, boyfriend or girlfriend, if you both have patience.

Just try flying off to Acapulco with the current sex symbol and see how well you get on if you are both impatient! For a few dazzling hours you may be able to conceal from one another the self-will lurking within. Even after the puzzled glances, the astonished stares, the little disagreements begin, you can still ignore them by searching out a new wine to savor, a new sight to see. But soon the truth becomes painfully clear to all parties, and before long you are on the phone: "Flight to the States, please — any flight! For one, one way."

When you are patient, on the other hand, an unkind word or thoughtless act will not agitate you. You will not want to run away or retaliate. Your support will hold steady, based as it is on deep respect and the knowledge that the Lord lives in the other person. Pride will not keep you from making the first — and, if need be, the second or third — overture towards reconciliation.

The scriptures of all religions contrast spiritual union with the relationship based solely on physical attraction. The first shows itself in patience and forgiveness; each person wants what is best for the other. The second cannot help being evanescent, marked by manipulation, self-assertion, and pride, because each person wants what is pleasurable for himself or herself.

We need not talk about right and wrong here at all. I am saying, simply and practically, that while sex has a beautiful place where loyalty exists, we cannot build a lasting relationship on it. The very nature of the physical bond is to exhaust itself quickly. One day we think Cecily or Algernon the most flawless, the most alluring creature on earth; we cannot live another moment apart from such embodied charm. This is the stuff of great literature — all those stories and poems which depict the suffering lover. But some months later, isn't most or all of that gone? Strange, but when we look closely, Cecily has some not so endearing quirks of personality that we never noticed before; Algernon's physical imperfections have begun to grate on our nerves. And there we are: alone again, lonely, perhaps moving on to Angelique or Zachary...who (and this time we couldn't be wrong) *is* the most flawless and alluring creature on earth.

I am not denying the temporary satisfaction in a relationship centered only on sex. That is what pulls us into it. But if we follow that pull, we are heading for disruption, and for all the heartbreak and turmoil that follow. If we want relationships that deepen with the passage of time, relationships that help us grow, we have to remain loyal through the bad times as well as the good, to accept the differences as well as the congruencies. This is what we learn to do when we try patiently to put the other person first.

WIDENING THE CIRCLE OF LOVE

Of course, this applies not only to couples but to children and parents, and to friends and friends. Hugh, for instance, likes movies that are tough, hard-boiled, realistic...intrigues of Washington and Wall Street, documentary techniques, clacking teletypes, stark photography. But he can still take his teenage daughter to a heart-tugging story of love triumphant over adversity—and he can enjoy himself, even if the film is all lace and flowers, slow-motion abandonment in gorgeous color, ever so mistily out of focus. He doesn't need to change his tastes; he can enjoy her enjoyment...catching the look in her eyes, hearing her sigh, discreetly passing her a hanky at the appropriate times. His world expands with this kind of sharing, and their relationship deepens and grows.

The magazines and newspapers we buy, the furniture we select, the place we go for a vacation—all these opportunities for graceful yielding! At a restaurant, Hugh can let Elaine choose and then announce, "I'll have that too." Or Elaine, if she is daring, can leave her menu unopened: "Hugh, why don't you order for me tonight?" Little things, but they help to free us, to lower the barriers of self-will a little so that we move closer to our partner, our children, our friends.

Even in jobs we can learn to see things through somebody else's eyes. If a friend agrees to help Hugh sheetrock the new room in his house, for example, they will very likely face two different approaches to the job. Joey always works slowly and methodically; Hugh likes to get the job *done*. Around two in the afternoon he can't help complaining to himself, "Joey, can't you *hurry*? I don't want to miss *The Wide World of Sports*!"

Rigid opinions on the job lead to tension and resentment. Sometimes the whole project comes to a halt, with one worker announcing that he can't take it any longer and storming out. I remember seeing a cartoon of two distinguished-looking scientists boarding a jet. One of them is saying, "All right — we'll go to Stockholm together. We'll sit at the banquet and be photographed together. But after we get the Nobel prize, I never want to see your ugly mug again!"

Usually, of course, there are a number of valid ways to do a job, and the idea that our way is best may reflect nothing more than habit. Rather than trying to have everyone be like us, we can learn to see differences as part of the richness of life. Work then becomes a marvelous opportunity to practice patience and rub off the sharp edges and corners of our personality that separate us from others. If co-workers can profit by doing things the way we do, very likely they will see this and change. When their ways are better than our own, we can gracefully follow their example.

MENDING ESTRANGEMENTS

More awesome, more daring, we can learn to expand our love to include even those with whom we are in enmity. Estrangements, as all of us know, can drag on for months or years, sometimes between blood relatives. Parents and children fall out with each other; brothers who rode tricycles together, built tree houses, played football, and took their dates to the prom together, no longer speak to each other because of a quarrel over money or property. Co-workers, neighbors, one-time friends become alienated without realizing the terrible impact it has on consciousness.

"But I have grievances," we may say, "legitimate grievances. Isn't it natural to react with anger to wrongs we have endured?" I agree: there is an inborn tendency in us to fight back or move away from people we dislike. Instinct is a powerful force; we are used to obeying it without question. But every such force in consciousness can be transformed. As human beings, all of us have the capacity to take our evolution into our own hands and act not compulsively, but from free choice. If we hate because we are hated, injure because we are injured, we have no freedom; instinct has thrust its fingers up inside us as if we were a child's puppet. One finger goes into the arm, and we find ourselves hurling a piece of crockery; another opens the mouth and wags the tongue, and we hear ourselves saying, "Drop dead!"

When we hate someone we are bound to that person, just as if we felt affection. Often we cannot stop thinking about what we wish we could say or do to him: "Wouldn't I like to give so-and-so a piece of my mind!" Little things make us think of that person; he may even appear in our dreams. What a paradox! Here is someone we cannot stand, someone we go out of our way to avoid, yet we carry him around with us constantly. Part of our mind conjures up his image – which may not correspond to reality at all – and another part of the mind, dwelling on that image, flies into a rage.

Almost every estrangement can be mended if one person involved is willing and able to forgive. How easy to repay in kind – "an eye for an eye, a tooth for a tooth"! But just try to reverse the course of your mind when anger breaks loose. The Buddha compares the furious mind to a runaway chariot: only those with courage and endurance can control it; the others, borne helplessly about, simply finger the reins.

When we forgive, we wipe the slate clean. We choose to live, not in remembrance of the past, but in the present. We choose to trust, rather than live in fear of the future. Past and future, those twin burdens, fall away, and here, in the present moment, we are free to love unconditionally, wholly.

How long should we do this when the other continues to provoke us? I remind you of Jesus' words:

> Then Peter came up and asked him, "Lord, how often am I to forgive my brother if he goes on wronging me? As many as seven times?" Jesus replied, "I do not say seven times; I say seventy times seven."

We must persevere in forgiveness; that is why it is so challenging. Jesus himself showed the height this can reach when he said from the cross, "Father, forgive them, for they know not what they do."

Forgiveness makes whole both the forgiven and the forgiver. The forgiven may start anew and do better henceforth, even turn about completely. The forgiver comes to realize that he or she has brought into play a profound spiritual law: in forgiving those who have wronged us, we forgive ourselves for our wrongs of the past. Even though we may have, through ignorance, committed many mistakes in life, these mistakes need not weigh heavily on our hearts if we have tried our best to free ourselves from ill will. When all ill will is extinguished, we find ourselves in our native state, which is love.

Sometimes our enmities are not based on wrongs done us at all. We might be hard put to explain exactly why a certain person irritates us so much. English has many colorful expressions for this: "He goes against my grain," "She gets my goat," "He makes my skin crawl." There just seems to be something – or everything – about the person we cannot take. We don't like his pace, her gestures, his speech, her taste in clothes. We don't want to see him, don't even want to hear her mentioned favorably. In such cases, the real source of irritation is not the other person. We are tyrannized by our conditioning – our likes and dislikes.

However hard it may be, we have to close the distance between us and those we do not like if we really want to grow spiritually. Often it means gritting your teeth, walking over, and trying to be friendly to someone you cannot stand. You may not be too successful at first; perhaps you can only stay five minutes before the inner screaming becomes more than you can bear. The next time, though, you do better. And gradually you learn to master your mind, which means that you can transform antipathy into sympathy at will.

ON FIRE WITH LOVE

This almost miraculous capacity is beautifully illustrated in the lives of the great men and women of God, though people like us are not expected to go so far. The extravagant young gallant Francis Bernardone of Assisi had always loathed and feared leprosy. Wandering about in his costly garments, he would never touch the lepers around his village, could scarcely bring himself to look at them; when a leper came to beg alms of him, though he would give, he always sent someone else to make the gift. He used to pass the leprosy sanatorium with averted face, his handkerchief over his nostrils.

But a powerful force was already working within Francis. One day he seemed to hear a promise deep in his consciousness: "All that you used to avoid will turn itself to great sweetness and exceeding joy." Soon after, riding on horseback across the plains of Umbria, he came upon a terribly disfigured leper. For an instant, the old, powerful revulsion swept through the young man. But then, from a deeper level, came a flash of realization: *This is my brother!* Francis climbed down, went up to the pitiful figure, and offered alms. As the leper reached out to take them, Francis knelt and kissed the fingers so wasted by disease: and as he did so, the chroniclers tell us, he felt flood through his being that promised sweetness and joy.

We began with the ego-bound human being; we have come to the man or woman who has risen above separateness to become universal, on fire with love for all. My plea is that none of us cease striving until we reach this unitary consciousness, when we live in the certitude that all life is one and that whatever we do has an effect, for good or ill, everywhere. This is the realization John

Donne conveys in those haunting lines:

> No man is an island, entire of itself; every man is a
> piece of the continent, a part of the main. If a clod be
> washed away by the sea, Europe is the less, as well as if
> a promontory were, as well as if a manor of thy friends
> or of thine own were. Any man's death diminishes me,
> because I am involved in mankind. And therefore never
> send to know for whom the bell tolls: it tolls for thee.

Spiritual Fellowship

IN SANSKRIT THERE is a pithy saying that was on the tip of my grandmother's tongue every year when school began. At the end of the day I would run home to tell her who I had been with and what we had done that day. "You don't have to tell me who you have been with," she would say. "I can tell."

"All right, Granny, who?"

She would proceed to name every one of them . . . and she was always right.

"Granny," I would ask in amazement, "how did you know?"

And she would reply, *"Samsargad doshaguna bhavanti"* – which means, roughly, "We become like those we hang out with."

Granny wasn't one to waste words, so it was only when I learned to meditate that I began to understand what she was trying to tell me. Much more than words or behavior, she was talking about character – the influences on the mind that shape the kind of person we are becoming, for better and for worse.

According to this ancient Sanskrit saying, what is good in us and what is bad, our strong points and our weak points alike, develop because of constant association. When we associate with calm people, we become calm; when we associate with agitated people, we become agitated. When we frequent the company of people who are wise, we become wiser; when our company is otherwise, we become otherwise too. It should be no surprise, then, that an essential part of the spiritual life is joining together with those who are spiritually minded, those who want to promote our growth and who want us to promote theirs.

This should not be considered a luxury or an indulgence. The Buddha would say that most people throw themselves into the river of life and float downstream, moved here and there by the current. But the spiritual aspirant must swim upstream, against the current of habit, familiarity, and ease. It is an apt image. We know how the salmon fights its way along, returning at last to its original home. Those who set out to change themselves are salmon swimming against the relentless flow of the selfish life. Truly, we need every bit of support we can get; we need friends, loyal companions on the journey. We have to do the swimming, of course; nobody else can do it for us. But there will be an easier and swifter passage if we can swim with those who encourage us, who set a strong pace and will not stop until they reach their destination. The burdens are shared, easing them; the joys are shared too, multiplying them.

In Sanskrit, this sharing is called *satsang*. The word derives from two smaller words: *sat*, meaning "the good" or "truth" or "reality," and *sanga*, meaning "group" or "association." Thus it signifies the seekers of the highest, banded together.

Every day devout Buddhists chant three phrases, one of which touches upon this fellowship of seekers. "I take refuge in the Buddha" — he who shows the way, the perfect reminder that nirvana, or liberation, is indeed possible here on this earth in our lifetime. "I take refuge in the dharma" – in the deepest law of our being, that all of us are one. "I take refuge in the sangha" – in the company of those who have come together for the supreme purpose of attaining liberation.

LIVING TOGETHER

I am told that people now want to be loners and live by themselves. If you ask why, they will say it is more convenient; they can do what they want, when they want, in the way they want. When they shuffle in the door from work, tired and edgy, they don't need to concern themselves with squabbling children; they can kick off their shoes and drop their clothes anywhere. No waiting to get into the bathroom; they can turn on the hot water – there is always plenty of it – put some bubble bath or their little yellow duck in the tub, and stay as long as they like. And when they have finished, there is no partner or roommate to listen to. They can fix the perfect martini, set the stereo to the volume they like, and pet the turtle in the terrarium, which is always grateful for any attention it can get. All this is called freedom. I call it sterility and the surest road to making ourselves more separate and self-willed.

You occasionally hear it said that spiritual aspirants should drop everything and set off for the woods, or go to India and wander about on the slopes of the Himalayas. But only through daily contact with people – not trees or brooks or deer – can we train ourselves to be selfless in personal relationships.

When we keep company with those who are spiritually minded, we help each other grow through mutual support and example.

Yet since we are all human, we give each other plenty of opportunity for developing patience too. Either way, we move forward. If things are going well, fine; we can look for new challenges. If they are not going well, we have the challenges right there in front of us. But none of this is possible if we live in isolation. How can a basketball player achieve excellence if he never touches a ball? Doesn't a ballerina have to put on her slippers and a pianist sit down to his Steinway? In like fashion, we need to be with people if we want to learn to live in harmony with them.

People sometimes tell me, "I'm living with my family, but it's a terrible place for the spiritual life. My father says meditation is hogwash, and my mother's afraid I'll turn into a zombie. Should I move out?" As a general rule, it is much better to stay. No matter what the initial reaction may be, no matter how much teasing or ridicule we may have to bear for a while, everyone responds deeply to the growth of goodness and wisdom in a child, a partner, or a parent. All of us begin meditating in less than ideal circumstances. But if we are giving our best to these eight basic disciplines, we can be sure we will get all the opportunity we need for spiritual development.

So if you live with your family, fine; if not, wherever practicable, live with friends. The important matter is the day-to-day involvement. It is not enough just to take a room in a big house and eat by yourself — a house where the only thing you ever say to anyone is, "Has the mail come?" Get to know your friends and the people you live with. Is there anyone you ought to know better? Ask about their work, studies, or projects. Exchange views about space probes or vitamin C or mulching or trends in fiction. You will come to realize that rich relationships with a number of people constitute one of the great blessings on this earth.

Some people sparkle when things go well for them but withdraw into a shell of isolation when things go poorly. But dwelling on yourself only keeps you stuck in depression. When you feel inclined to brood, that is precisely the time to come out and be with people – to turn yourself outwards and away from your problems, which isolation only magnifies and distorts like a funhouse mirror.

THE SPIRITUAL HOUSEHOLD

Spiritual aspirants can share their lives in many ways. To begin with, if circumstances permit, invite friends from other households to join you in meditation. They can walk or ride over in the early morning and take their places beside you. Perhaps they can have breakfast there too, and leave with you for work or school. You might also try having dinner first at one house, then at another; you can stay on together for meditation later. Of course, some sacrifices may be needed. You may have to get up earlier, or skip a few activities in the evening. But the home where this occurs will become a better place to be. It takes some personal experience to understand why. If the neighbors were to glance in and see everybody seated there – still, silent, eyes closed – they probably would not grasp that spiritually those people are moving closer moment by moment.

After a time, the room set aside for meditation will become valued by all. Where before the television room or kitchen was the hub of bustling life, now the meditation room, though only used for a portion of the day, symbolizes the growing harmony in the house. Little by little, that room becomes holy.

Once or twice a week, you might spend an evening with your spiritual companions reading and discussing the scriptures and the writings of the mystics. Most of the spiritual documents mentioned in the next chapter can be used, but I would especially suggest *The Bhagavad Gita for Daily Living*. In this commentary on one of the world's great scriptures, I have included many practical suggestions for applying the eight-point program presented in this book. I think you will find that it is not an arid or philosophical presentation, but one meant to touch your day-to-day life.

The mantram too fits in perfectly with family and friends. For instance, you can have a brief period of quiet for repeating the mantram before meals, bringing all to a remembrance of the company, the loving preparation of the food, and the divine Giver of it. And why not bring the mantram along on outings, repeating it silently instead of distracting the driver with unnecessary talk? You can watch the scenery while you do; you don't have to close your eyes. Repeating the mantram will also help overcome the ups and downs of those annual family vacations where everyone piles into the car full of excitement and comes back ten days later hot and tired, drooping and deflated, with a few stickers on the dusty windows proclaiming that they did indeed make it to the mystery caves and the petrified forest.

Slowing down and practicing one-pointed attention benefit from the support of others. When people around you are reading at the table — the sports page, a chemistry text, "Dear Abby," and the stock quotations — it is difficult not to fall into the habit. But when most are giving their full attention to the meal and the company, we naturally do the same. Similarly, if we find ourselves starting to rush about in the kitchen because special guests are expected, it is much easier to slow down again if the rest of the household is maintaining a leisurely pace.

Mealtime, of course, is the most natural time for good companionship. How fulfilling to eat food cooked with love in the midst of those we love and who love us! Think of that poignant gathering, the Last Supper, the simple scene of Jesus giving his final instructions and bidding farewell to his disciples over bread shared by all. Every meal should be a sacrament, in which we strengthen not only the body but the spirit too.

But if the meal is to be sacramental, the home must be a loving one. Today it has often become an institution where people with different interests take their meals and sleep. Everyone wants to be on the move; no one can find a minute to be with anyone else. We seem to live in giant centrifuges that hurl us out at every opportunity for our shopping trips, dance lessons, club meetings, bowling leagues, and overtime work at the office. I am sometimes asked if I think a woman's place is in the home. I reply, "Of course. And a man's place is in the home, too."

To make a meal a time of sharing, we should avoid all acrimonious talk. How ironic that when the whole household gathers — perhaps only once a day — we often make remarks which drive us apart and spoil our digestion! Mealtime is no time to quarrel about hairstyles or hem lengths, to recriminate with someone for not doing an errand, or to dispute about foreign policy. On the other hand, we are not sharing when we sit in deathly silence, each person entombed in his own concerns, issuing forth only for an occasional "Pass the butter, please."

Instead of looking at a meal as a chore, as something to be hurried over or an opportunity to settle grievances, we can come to see it as a precious time of communion. We extend this time when all who are able join in preparing the food. If there is a household vegetable garden, and perhaps some fruit trees, everyone can participate in growing the food too. Even small families can plant, care for, and harvest some of what they eat; they share the labor, and they share the bounty. Children of all ages delight in tending living things; it teaches them about growth, nurturing, and the cycles of nature.

When it comes to training the senses, spiritual fellowship is crucial. If you go out with an undiscriminating crowd and pass a dimly remembered haunt, you may well find yourself seated again in your favorite corner with a mug of lukewarm beer and the last few pretzels in front of you, watching the proprietor turn the chairs upside down on the tabletops and wondering where the evening went. It is hard to say no to a group, even hard to say no to one coaxing friend. But if you are with spiritually minded companions, they will know what you're up against, and vice versa. You can steer right around each other's temptations and together find some tasty, healthful food to eat, some entertaining, worthwhile things to do.

RECREATION

In their earnestness, some people who take to the spiritual life devalue recreation. But the spiritual life should not be grim. It should be lighthearted, and recreation has an important place. If we have been working hard, the body needs to be renewed and the mind refreshed. When we spend leisure time with our family or friends on a picnic or a trip to the beach, that is spiritual fellowship. But it is not necessary to go as far as the beach.

Why not go for an evening walk repeating the mantram? You will probably see a few things you had never really noticed; perhaps you will have a chance to talk a bit with the neighbors or their children too.

If a good movie comes along – always at least a possibility – go together to see it. A play, especially a musical that the children will enjoy, is ideal, even if the company consists of local high school students who haven't perfected their talents in singing and dancing. The lights, costumes, sets, and actual presence of the performers will give the children, and the grown-ups too, what the silver screen never can. We share something special when the audience and the performers come together in the same place at the same time.

We don't even have to leave the house to entertain ourselves. For millions, of course, entertainment at home means only one thing, television. How we have let ourselves be enslaved by those alluring displays! I suggest that you turn it off, consider getting rid of it, and try some participatory recreation in your own home or backyard. Especially if there are children in your household, try reading aloud from stories and plays. Memorize a few lines or hold the text or just improvise – add a few old clothes, some makeup, a wig, a mustache or two, and you're on stage. But however you do it, be active. Let us not accept as entertainment those half-hour, prefabricated television programs and lose our capacity to entertain ourselves.

SPIRITUAL SEEDLINGS

The transformation of personality is so difficult that to accomplish it we cannot afford to dedicate ourselves to other objectives and try to practice spiritual disciplines on the side. In the early days, however, this often means a change in some of our familiar activities. Old acquaintances may gradually fade from our circle. To rebuild our lives, we have to change our associations and our ways of living.

When I say we need to be selective in our company, however, I am not talking about withdrawing into a little group and refusing to have any contact with people who do not do as we do. We should be courteous and friendly with everyone, aware of their feelings and points of view, and avoid being judgmental. I am stressing the need to build deep relationships with those who welcome the changes we are trying to make and who will help us make them.

When a seedling is planted in the countryside, it is fenced in so it will have some protection. Similarly, as spiritual seedlings, it is a good idea to surround ourselves with the protection of others who are spiritually minded. In time, of course, when our new ways of thought, speech, and action have taken a firm hold, we can stand in any company without being uprooted. Far from returning to our old patterns of conditioning, we will influence others by our personal example to change their patterns as well.

This can be painful at first. When I took to meditation I made a number of far-reaching changes in my life, which naturally baffled a lot of my friends, who began to look askance at some of these changes. They were fond of me and thought perhaps I was losing my ambition and my drive. What I did was to try not to be affected by this, not in any way to be apologetic or to impose my views on others. In a few years' time they saw the changes I had been able to bring into my daily living and one by one they would seek my company, perhaps even to ask my advice on daily problems.

If you are following my eight-point program, therefore, my practical suggestion would be to make time to meditate as often as possible with others on the same path. You may read together for a short while or watch one of our videos, but the most important part is meditation. Wherever people meditate together, a healing force is released that deepens the experience for all. As Jesus says, "Where two or three are gathered together in my name, I am present in the midst of them."

One of the important reasons for our Blue Mountain Center retreats is to provide this kind of rendezvous, where people who are searching for the supreme purpose of life can support one another and share companionship on this demanding journey. I am always pleased to hear from friends that our retreats are like an oasis for them, where they can find living waters and return home refreshed.

LOFTY COMPANIONSHIP

But we also need transcendent companionship. The highest form of spiritual association is with someone who embodies our highest ideals and aspirations, someone we want to be like in every possible way. It might be Jesus or the Compassionate Buddha; it might be a great saint like Sri Ramakrishna, Francis of Assisi, Teresa of Avila, or Thérèse of Lisieux.

This does not require a physical presence. Jesus, the Buddha, great sages and saints like Sri Ramakrishna, Mahatma Gandhi, Teresa of Avila, Francis of Assisi, all continue to guide us. They are not dead. Their bodies are gone, but their spirit moves about freely in the world, helping those who turn to them with a unified heart.

Similarly, my teacher is much more real to me today than she was when I was a child. And for Francis and Teresa, Jesus was a friend with whom they conversed intimately, just as Sri Ramakrishna did with the Divine Mother.

Even for people like you and me, luminous figures like these in every religion can be living companions — much more real, much more influential, than flesh and blood friends whose lives are scattered. By reading about them, thinking about them, meditating on their words, we can bring their presence into our daily lives.

Wherever people gather for selfless ends, there is a vast augmentation of their individual capacities. Something wonderful, something momentous happens. An irresistible force begins to move, which, though we may not see it, is going to change our world. In this lies the power and the meaning of spiritual fellowship.

Spiritual Reading

THE SPIRITUAL LIFE is so arduous, so challenging, that it can be likened to an ascent up a lofty and noble mountain. We start from the plains — we might even say Death Valley — and slowly, very slowly, work our way up. There are joyous recompenses, of course: knowing that at long last we are moving towards the summit, glancing back and seeing how far we have come, feeling ever stronger and more vibrantly alive. But there are difficulties too, and they do not disappear as we climb higher. Gorges fall away on all sides, massive rocks stand in our pathway and must be surmounted, swirling mists and storms impair our vision. Cold and lonely seems the way at times, and we doubt we will ever reach the top.

At such moments we can draw welcome consolation from the writings of the mystics who have themselves gone up this mountain. Whenever our confidence ebbs — for most of us as frequently as the ebbing of the sea — we can turn to the words of these men and women of God and renew our hearts, draw fresh breath, and bring back into sight our supreme goal. Their trials put our obstacles into perspective, and their triumphs give us courage. We see just what we can be as human beings: our capacity to choose, to change, to endure, to know, to love, to radiate spiritual glory. Personally, I never tire of reading these precious documents. How blessed it is to be in the holy presence of a Saint Teresa or a Sri Ramakrishna!

When I first came to this country I brought on shipboard the unabridged version of *The Gospel of Sri Ramakrishna,* over a thousand pages, and I spent many, many hours poring over it. True, I missed out on my chance to eat six or seven meals a day, sharpen up my shuffleboard skills, and doze in a rainbow deck chair. I immersed myself instead in that great book, which provided a timely answer to every spiritual question I asked. It isn't even necessary to read the *Gospel* systematically. At almost every page words speak to our condition, strengthen us, and console us.

THE NATURE OF MYSTICAL LITERATURE

Mystical literature differs from other forms of writing in that as our understanding deepens, we draw more from it. Most books are not like that. We exhaust our interest in a murder mystery once we discover that the butler's uncle did it, and even a fine novel is circumscribed by the awareness of the author. But there is no limit to the profundity of spiritual writings, because they have come from those whose consciousness has merged with the infinite. We take away as much as we can carry.

I do need to sound a few cautions about spiritual reading, though. Many of us are so intellectually oriented that we can easily misunderstand its purpose. Spiritual reading is meant to inspire us to change and show us how to change, but I feel sure the mystics themselves would agree — some having learned it through trial and error — that reading cannot be substituted for experience. No matter how many mystics we read, we cannot move forward on the spiritual path without practicing their teachings in daily life.

A hard admonition for some of us. One contemporary thinker put it very well when he remarked that if we had to choose between uniting ourselves with God and hearing a lecture about it, most of us would hunt for a good seat. I must admit that I myself once believed that all knowledge lay between two endpapers, and I responded to the smell of a newly printed book just as a gourmet responds to the smell of a piquant sauce. I delighted in opening a new acquisition carefully, admiring the printing and binding, and looking forward to the moment when I would be able to settle into my easy chair, open to chapter one, and drink in its wisdom. I have since learned to be more discriminating.

I once visited the home of a well-known writer on spiritual themes who took me into his exceptionally full library. There were books on every conceivable kind of meditation, really an impressive collection. "With all these books on the subject," I said, "you must be an adept in meditation."

He looked a little embarrassed, "Frankly," he said, "I'm so busy reading and studying that I don't have time to meditate."

Then he pulled down some of his favorites from the shelves. "You must be familiar with all of these."

I too looked a little embarrassed. "Only a few." I did not want to say so, but instead of reading about meditation, I had used my time to practice it.

If you want to know the mystical tradition, don't rely on books about the mystics; go directly to the great mystics themselves. A scholarly presentation may have its place, but personal testimonies are infinitely more helpful. When I was a student of English literature, we were expected to know a great deal about Shakespeare's plays: Hamlet's motivation, the psychology of Lady Macbeth, the kinds of comedy in *A Midsummer Night's Dream*. How many books I read by how many scholars, critics, producers, theater historians, actors — all of it *about* Shakespeare; scores and scores of books from secondary perspectives. I read what Richards thought about Bradley's comment on Coleridge's opinion of Dryden's evaluation of Shakespeare in his "Essay of Dramatic Poesy." Endless! Only later did I realize that by poring over the words of Shakespeare himself, I could have penetrated into the characters, the plot twists, the poetry, the very texture of the plays and of Shakespeare's spirit. But I did not know this at the time; I probably lacked the confidence to put it into practice. Only after I learned to meditate and began to trust my own powers of observation did I see that I had mistaken a packet of maps for the land.

So please read the words of Saint Augustine and don't do what I did with the Bard and read what A claims B said C thought about Saint Augustine. The opportunities to detour increase all the time; so many books on the spiritual life are available, an overwhelming array. Don't spend time on faint reflections; go directly to the sources of radiance.

Books chosen from the annals of mysticism should be read slowly and well. We are not after information, but understanding and inspiration. Take in a little every day, reflect on it, and then try to practice what you have learned.

There is a tale of a man who found on the road a large stone bearing the words, "Under me lies a great truth." The man strained to turn the stone over and finally succeeded. On the bottom was written, "Why do you want a new truth when you do not practice what you already know?"

In spiritual reading, too, it takes time to assimilate the truths we meet. Far better to read a few books and make them your own than to read many books quickly and superficially — just as you will grow more crops by cultivating your own garden, however tiny, than by flying in an airplane over all the farmland in the county.

AN EVENING ROUTINE

I have found spiritual reading especially beneficial after evening meditation. When I have finished, I go to bed and repeat the mantram until I fall asleep in it. The reason for this sequence is simple: what we put into consciousness in the evening goes with us into sleep. If we use this valuable time to fill our mind with agitating stuff from books, movies, or television shows, that is what we will see and hear in our dreams. On the other hand, if we follow this nightly sequence of meditation, spiritual reading, and repetition of the mantram, our dreams will gradually reflect an evening wisely spent. We will grow in patience, security, wisdom even while we sleep.

I suggest, then, that you include half an hour's reading every day, preferably at night. If this is not possible, have fifteen minutes. Probably you will soon want more time for such reading. It will become something you hunger for — rather like your dinner, which I am sure you don't care to miss.

In this, as with other things, we should observe what the Buddha called the middle path. It helps to have some spiritual reading every day so that our enthusiasm does not flag, but we should use our discrimination too. It would certainly be a mistake to pull away from our work, family, or other obligations to shut ourselves up in a room with books, no matter how inspiring they may be.

READ WIDELY

The treasures of mysticism can be found in all religions, and we should not confine ourselves to the tradition most familiar to us. No one age, no one people, no one persuasion has any monopoly on spiritual wisdom; the prize is there, and always has been, for any man or woman who cares and dares to look for it.

Of course, whichever mystic we turn to, we will meet the same truths, because the mystical experience is everywhere the same. There is only one supreme reality, and there can be only one union with it. But the language, tradition, mode of expression, and cultural flavor will differ. One writes in French, another in Pali. One writes in poetry, another in prose. One speaks of the Mother, another of His Majesty, still another of the Beloved. In this lies the beauty of spiritual literature: on the one hand it reflects the fascinating diversity of life; on the other, the unchanging principles that stand behind that diversity, irrespective of time and place.

Here, however, it is helpful to draw a practical distinction. On the one hand, there are books we read primarily for inspiration. They can be glorious, we need them, but taken together they encompass diverse ideas, disciplines, and methods of meditation. If we try to follow the exact letter of what we read — say, this week the Hasidic masters, next week Saint Anthony — we will be dancing and singing for seven days and living on bread and water for the next seven. So the other kind of spiritual reading I call instructional — the works which actually bring us the detailed advice of our spiritual teacher. We should draw freely on the classics of all great mystical traditions for inspiration, but this should never take the place of reading and rereading the instructions we are trying to follow in our daily lives.

Sometimes, when I look back over the books I have written, I think how much easier it would have been for me if such books had been available when I was learning to meditate. And that is why I have written them: to support those who are trying to put this eight-point program into practice. They are based entirely on personal experience, and their sole purpose is to help readers make their highest ideals a part of their daily lives.

I have said many times that Saint Francis lives in the words of his prayer. Gandhi may be said to live in the second chapter of the Gita, on which he based his life. Similarly, you can say that I live in my eight-point program, and I can assure you that I live in my audio and video recordings for those who are practicing my method of meditation to the best of their ability and following the instructions faithfully with an open heart. You have to remember that when I started to meditate, my own spiritual teacher, my grandmother, had already passed away. At first I felt very much on my own, but at every stage, when I turned to her for guidance, I found answers to my questions. So if you are following this method of meditation, I would encourage you to read my books over and over and follow the instructions on meditation very carefully.

SOME GREAT DOCUMENTS

We can see the universality of the mystical outlook, and the individuality of the mystics too, by surveying a few writings I have found to be especially helpful to spiritual aspirants. Let us begin with the Western tradition. In their enthusiasm for the East, many people in the Western world today overlook the breadth and depth of the mystical writings from their own traditions. There *are* grand books from the East, and they should be read, but why confuse spiritual insight with the exotic trappings in which it seems to the foreign eye to be dressed? Actually, I have encountered this in both worlds. Some of my friends in India, especially the younger ones, clamor for Western things; it all looks so novel and appealing from a distance, very heady stuff. And in this country, one just has to mention mandalas or Tai Chi or tantra yoga to turn heads. A little of this attitude is harmless enough, but when it causes us to forget the excellence of our own heritage, we suffer a real loss.

The Christian tradition has brought forth many great saints who have left accounts of their growth in consciousness. One who appeals to me deeply is Saint Teresa of Avila, whose three books — *The Autobiography, The Way of Perfection,* and *The Interior Castle* — chronicle nearly twenty years of spiritual apprenticeship which transformed this young woman, unrivaled for her beauty and accomplishments, into a humble servant of her Lord. Teresa also left a few short poems, stamped with her own experience, which make inspiring passages for meditation. This one shows her simplicity and her capacity to penetrate straight to the essence:

Let nothing upset you;
Let nothing frighten you.
Everything is changing;
God alone is changeless.
Patience attains the goal.
Who has God lacks nothing:
God alone fills all our needs.

In the last hundred years another woman with the same name, Saint Thérèse of Lisieux, popularly known as the "Little Flower," has won the hearts of readers everywhere. Thérèse, canonized in 1925, died at twenty-four and left the world only one book from her own hand, *The Story of a Soul.* Her immense appeal is due largely to what she once called her "little way": the thousand and one small acts of kindness toward family and friends by which we learn to forget ourselves in the joy and welfare of the whole. Thérèse's endearing combination of naivete and spiritual daring comes through vividly in this passage from *The Story of a Soul,* in which she describes how she learned to love a nun in her convent whom she found "disagreeable in every way":

Not wanting to give in to the natural antipathy I was feeling, I told myself that love should consist not in sentiments but in action. Then I applied myself to do for this sister just what I would do for the person I love most...I tried to render her every possible service, and when I was tempted to answer her in a disagreeable way, I contented myself with giving her my friendliest smile and tried to change the subject...As she was absolutely ignorant of how I

felt for her,... she told me one day with a contented
air, almost in these very words: "Would you tell me,
Sister Thérèse, what attracts you so much towards me?
Each time you see me I see you smiling." Ah! What
attracts me is Jesus, hidden in the depths of her soul —
Jesus who makes sweet that which is most bitter...

Another practical manual of spiritual instruction comes to us
from a man known as Brother Lawrence. At the age of eighteen
he chanced to see a bare tree silhouetted against the gray sky,
and the realization that it would burgeon again in full glory in
the spring brought a deep and lasting awareness of the power of
God. He entered a Carmelite monastery, where of course he was
expected to join other monks at their work. Lawrence tells us that
he had always had an aversion for anything connected with the
preparation of food. Inwardly, I suppose, he must have said to
his superiors, "Let me work in the stable or on the grounds. Let
me illuminate manuscripts. But, please, not the kitchen." So they
put him in the kitchen — not from callousness, but to help him go
beyond his likes and dislikes, knowing that peace of mind cannot depend on external circumstances. Brother Lawrence was
installed among the pots and pans, salads and sauces, while the
brother who loved to cook and could turn out a perfect soufflé
was probably sent to the laundry room.

Then a wonderful transformation took place. With a great
effort spanning a number of years, Lawrence strove to remember the presence of God at every moment, even in the kitchen.
When at last he achieved that remembrance, he came to say that
he was as close to the Lord amidst the clatter and confusion of

his pots and pans as when he knelt for prayer in the chapel. You can read his simple, practical advice in his book, *The Practice of the Presence of God.*

Since its first printed edition in 1472, *Of the Imitation of Christ* by Thomas à Kempis has been, excepting the Bible, the most widely read religious book in the Christian world. It is not a narrative but a book of spiritual counsel, an "introduction to the devout life." Listen to what it has to say about love:

> ...by itself it makes light everything that is heavy, and bears evenly all that is uneven. For it carries a burden that is no burden, and makes everything that is bitter, sweet and tasteful... Love feels no burden, thinks nothing of trouble, attempts what is above its strength, pleads no excuse of impossibility... Though weary, it is not tired; though pressed, it is not straitened; though alarmed, it is not confounded; but like a lively flame and burning torch forces its way upwards and securely passes through all... In whatever instance we seek ourselves, there we fall from love.

This whole chapter – "On the Wonderful Effect of Divine Love" – makes a perfect passage for meditation. There are other inspiring selections also, but in reading the *Imitation* or selecting passages from it, we need to keep a few things in mind. Thomas was a monk for over seventy years, and he sometimes uses an idiom appropriate for the monastic order but not for householders. As a novice-master, he advised his charges to forget the world they had left behind. Our goal, on the other hand, is to be "in the world but not of it": to strive to move gracefully among all the activities of daily life without being ensnared by either outer things or inner desires.

Also, in medieval fashion, Thomas tends to compare human beings to God – rather at our expense. We should remember, though, that what is ignoble about human nature is not our true Self – ever pure, never sullied by any thought, word, or deed – but the usurping ego who has taken over the kingdom of consciousness. This rude fellow is not the real "I." He can and must be pulled down from the throne where he arrogantly issues his self-serving orders and banished forever, allowing the true Self to take its rightful place and rule in splendor once again. John Woolman, a Quaker mystic in colonial America, records his experience of this coronation in his *Diary*:

In a time of sickness with the pleurisy...I was brought so near the gates of death that I forgot my name. Being then desirous to know who I was, I saw a mass of matter of a dull gloomy color between the South and the East, and was informed that this mass was human beings in as great misery as they could be, and live, and that I was mixed with them, and that henceforth I might not consider myself as a distinct or separate being. In this state I remained several hours. I then heard a soft melodious voice, more pure and harmonious than any voice I had heard with my ears before; and I believed it was the voice of an angel who spoke to other angels. The words were, *John Woolman is dead*. I soon remembered that I was once John Woolman and being assured that I was alive in the body, I greatly wondered what that heavenly voice could mean...At length I felt divine power prepare my mouth that I could speak, and then said, "I am crucified with Christ, nevertheless, I live; yet not I, but Christ liveth in me. And the life I now live in the flesh is by faith in the Son of God who loved me and gave himself for me." Then the mystery was opened, and I perceived that there was joy in heaven over a sinner who had repented, and that language, *John Woolman is dead*, meant no more than the death of my own will.

The Way of a Pilgrim is the tale of an anonymous Russian peasant, a humble and simple soul. With a couple of holy books and a little bread in his knapsack, this homeless man with a crippled arm roams the towns and wilds of nineteenth-century Russia repeating the Jesus Prayer. Dark times befall him: he is robbed, nearly freezes to death, is falsely accused of crime. But there are times of spiritual brightness too, when he sits by his teacher, when he is befriended by loving and devout Christians, when he does a good turn for the very men who robbed him. The whole story makes vivid the power to be found in the repetition of the holy name.

In Judaism, parts of the holy scriptures and traditional liturgies contain the most sublime poetry for meditation:

In this moment of silent communion with Thee, O Lord, a still small voice speaks in the depth of my spirit. It speaks to me of the things I must do to attain holy kinship with Thee and to grow in the likeness of Thee. I must do my allotted task with unflagging faithfulness even though the eye of no taskmaster

is on me. I must be gentle in the face of ingratitude
or when slander distorts my noblest motives. I must
come to the end of each day with a feeling that I have
used its gifts gratefully and faced its trials bravely.

O Lord, help me to be ever more like Thee, holy
for Thou art holy, loving for Thou art love.

Speak to me, then, Lord, as I seek Thee again
and again in the stillness of meditation, until
Thy bidding shall at last become for me a
hallowed discipline, a familiar way of life.

For centuries too the mystics of Islam — men and women like
Ansari of Herat, Jalaluddin Rumi, Fariduddin Attar, Rabi'a, Mah-
mud Shabestari, Sheikh Abu Sa'id — have been praising the Lord
in magnificent language. Here is Abu Sa'id:

If you want to draw near to God,
seek him in the hearts of those around you.
Speak well of all, present or absent.
If you would be a light for others,
be like the sun: show the same face to all.

To bring joy to a single heart is better
than building countless shrines for worship;
to capture one heart through kindness
is better than setting a thousand free.

This is the true lover of God,
who lives with others,

rises and eats and sleeps like others,
gives and takes with others in the bazaar,
yet never forgets God even for a moment.

Buddhism has a venerable tradition of mystical writings; above all, I would recommend the Dhammapada. Its twenty-six chapters distill the essence of the Buddha's teachings and bear the stamp of his personal experience. The Buddha was a spiritual scientist with a penetrating intellect, relentlessly logical in his pursuit of truth. Using homely images that the villagers of ancient India could easily grasp — no less vivid for us today — he presents the human condition as incisively as an experienced physician. The diagnosis: raging desire, possibly terminal. The antidote: nirvana, the extinction of all selfishness. The prognosis: hopeful, excellent. And last, as we would expect from a good doctor, a strong but invigorating medicine to ensure recovery: the Noble Eightfold Path, based on the practice of meditation.

In *Footprints of Gautama the Buddha,* Marie Byles presents the life of the Buddha as it might have been seen by an early disciple. Drawn from ancient documents, this lively narrative is peopled with some fascinating characters. It makes a good book for reading aloud to youngsters — but be prepared for some gulps and big eyes at the point where the Buddha comes face to face with the terror of the countryside, the fierce bandit Angulimala.

Hinduism embraces a vast and diverse collection of scriptures and mystical writings, some of them going back many thousands of years. The Upanishads, the oldest of these, are among the most profound of all spiritual documents. Over one hundred Upanishads have come down to us, and of these, ten or so are generally regarded as the principal ones. I have translated these and a few others in *The Upanishads,* part of my Classics of Indian Spirituality series; they make ideal passages for use in meditation.

To me, the Katha stands as one of the most significant of all the Upanishads. In it a teenager named Nachiketa goes to the abode of Yama, the King of Death. There, as a gesture of hospitality, Death offers him three boons. Would he like long life? Gold and jewels? Kingdoms and power? Nachiketa, the perfect spiritual aspirant, responds that all this will someday fall into the hands of Death. "Give me something permanent," he says, "something beyond your grasp." Yama, pleased, gives the boy instruction into the mysteries of death and immortality.

Those interested in the theory and practice of meditation might turn to the classic text, Patanjali's *Yoga Sutras.* Patanjali was a brilliant teacher of meditation in ancient India who brought together what earlier sages had learned about the mind and its mastery — rather a lot! — and arranged it all in a priceless handbook noted for the scientific rigor of its presentation. Patanjali's work is as condensed as a professor's lecture notes, for it was intended to be filled out, interpreted, and commented on by an experienced teacher. There are many editions, but the one I recommend is *How to Know God: The Yoga Aphorisms of Patanjali,* by Swami Prabhavananda and Christopher Isherwood. This commentary, aimed at a sincere Western audience, combines practicality with the insight of deep spiritual experience.

Earlier I mentioned *The Gospel of Sri Ramakrishna,* the one volume I brought with me when I came to this country. It was written by a retired schoolmaster totally devoted to Sri Ramakrishna, the tremendous mystic of nineteenth-century Bengal. This school-master, who modestly signed himself "M," loved his teacher so deeply that he would sit in his little room after the sun set and write down from memory everything that had been said by the Master and his disciples and guests, sometimes from morning till evening. The result is an extraordinary achievement which Aldous Huxley called the greatest piece of hagiographic literature in the world, full of lively parables, lucid explanations of difficult spiritual matters, and dazzling accounts of mystical union. If you take this book up, I don't think you will want to part from it. If the background seems strange at first, Christopher Isherwood's *Ramakrishna and His Disciples* makes a perfect introduction.

Of all the books from any spiritual tradition, none has meant more to me than the Bhagavad Gita. If I may borrow Gandhi's words, "It became my dictionary of daily reference. Just as I turned to the English dictionary for the meanings of English words that I did not understand, I turned to this dictionary of conduct for a ready solution of all my troubles and trials." To make the Gita more accessible to modern readers, I have offered my own translation and practical commentary in *The Bhagavad Gita for Daily Living,* drawing on personal experience to show how the precepts of the Gita can be put to work in our own lives.

The eighteen chapters of the Gita pursue a dialogue between the young prince Arjuna, who stands for you and me, and the Lord himself, in the form of Sri Krishna. Arjuna has many questions, many reservations, many doubts; his divine teacher patiently sets them to rest. One passage at the end contains the quintes-sence of spiritual wisdom. Arjuna wants to know the nature of those who have scaled the peaks of human consciousness. For those of us making this daring ascent, the Lord's answer, like the sure words of a perfect guide, reminds us of what we shall be once we reach the summit:

Unerring in discrimination,
Sovereign of the senses and passions,
Free from the clamor of likes and dislikes,
They lead a simple, self-reliant life
Based on meditation, using speech,
Body, and mind to serve the Lord of Love.

Free from self-will, aggression, arrogance,
From the lust to possess people or things,
They are at peace with themselves and others
And enter into the unitive state.

United with the Lord, ever joyful,
Beyond the reach of self-will and sorrow,
They see me in every living creature
And attain supreme devotion to me.

By loving me they share in my glory
And enter into my boundless being.
All their acts are performed in my service,
And through my grace they win eternal life.

May each of you, through ceaseless striving and the infinite grace and love of him who is the source of all, realize this blessed state!

Part II. Questions and Answers

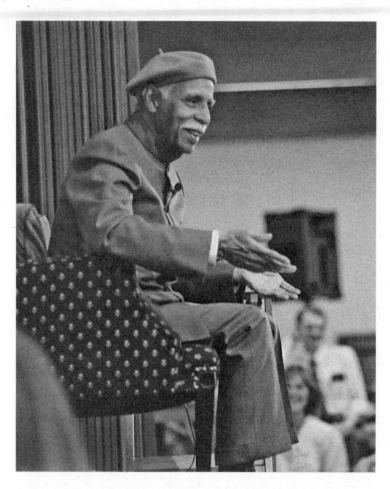

During his forty years as a teacher of meditation, Eknath Easwaran regularly held question and answer sessions. Many questions came up over and over, as they still do today in the retreats offered by the Blue Mountain Center of Meditation. Here are some of those questions together with Easwaran's answers.

Meditation

There are so many methods of meditation available today that I get confused. Could you explain what you understand by meditation?

First, meditation as I teach and practice it is not a relaxation technique. I respect teachers and health professionals who use the word in this way, but we have the testimony of great mystics from every culture and every age that meditation requires strenuous effort.

Second, although there are highly respectable schools of meditation which rightly emphasize that their goal is not relaxation but awareness, their methods often involve heightening awareness of some physiological activity like breathing. I respect these methods in the hands of an experienced teacher, but to me meditation is essentially an interior discipline. The mind needs to turn inward, and to do this we have to forget the body during the period of meditation. (Interestingly enough, it is just when we forget about the body that it functions at its best.)

Third, meditation as I teach it is not visualization, nor is it drifting in a reverie and imagining pleasant things. It is not letting the mind wander, "guided" or unguided, nor observing thoughts flow by in quiet detachment. If we could really watch our thoughts in that manner, our emotions would have no power to seize hold of us — which means we would never lose our temper, never think a hostile thought, never feel afraid.

Finally, it is important to distinguish meditation from disciplined reflection on a particular theme. I stress this because many eminent spiritual figures have used the word in this way. Reflection on a spiritual topic can yield valuable insights; but for the vast majority of us, reflection is an activity on the surface level of the mind. To transform personality we need to go much, much deeper. We need a way to get eventually into the unconscious itself, where our contrary thoughts and deepest desires arise, and make changes there. That is the purpose of meditation.

Meditation, then, means training the mind: teaching our thoughts to go where we tell them and to obey themselves while they are there, much as we train a puppy. We begin by learning how to train our attention — both in meditation and during the rest of the day — until eventually we make our mind calm, clear, and concentrated as a laser, which we can direct and focus at will. When you have this kind of mastery over your attention in everything you do, you have a genius for life itself: unshakable security, clear judgment, deep personal relationships, compassion that no adversity can break down.

Could you say more about the practical benefits?

This method of meditation is really a program for the whole of the day. All the eight points of this program work together, and all are aimed at the training of attention, both during the period of meditation itself and during the rest of the day.

The value of this is that if you can succeed in training your attention to a great extent, you can deal with most of the emotional problems in life. Little things that should be treated as pinpricks grow to be serious problems not because they are serious in themselves but because of the continuing attention they receive when we dwell on them. Training attention enables you to turn your attention away from that problem to something more positive, more promising.

In other words, it's very much like changing channels on TV. When you don't like something on TV, you can change to something worth watching – and when you don't find anything worth watching, you can turn the TV off. That is the final achievement in training attention. When our attention is caught in something unproductive, such as worrying or replaying old resentments or regrets, we can just switch the program off.

To change the metaphor, just as you park your car and turn off the engine at the end of the day, you can learn to park your attention. And just as turning off the engine saves gas, when you park your attention, all the vital energy that is used in worrying and dwelling and brooding on the negative aspects of life is conserved. That is why meditation brings more energy, more drive, more confidence that you are up to life's challenges.

The practical benefits of this are immense. Everybody in the world knows that we react to people. If you are angry, I am angry. If you dislike me, I dislike you. If you avoid me, I avoid you. And my teacher used to say, "Do you want to be like a tennis ball, which obeys the racquet? Don't you want to live in freedom?" Control over your attention brings freedom. You no longer react; you can choose your response. You lose the capacity to be angry

186 · QUESTIONS AND ANSWERS

against angry people, to move away from people who move away from you. Eventually you even lose the capacity to think negatively, to have any kind of ill will against anybody at all. And as our ancient scriptures say, when all capacity for ill will is gone, what is left is original goodness. When all capacity for hatred is gone, what is left is original love.

Do I have to change my beliefs in order to practice passage meditation?

Meditation can be practiced in every religion, and without professing any religion at all. It is not a dogma or a belief; it is a dynamic, tremendously powerful discipline, a mighty tool that can be mastered by anybody with daring and drive. In fact, I would say that training the mind to be calm, clear, and compassionate under all circumstances is the very essence of religion.

I want to try your method of meditation, but I also want to stay loyal to my religious tradition.

This method of meditation is based on inspirational passages from the world's great scriptures and mystics, so it fits perfectly into any religious tradition. You can choose to meditate on passages only from your religion, but I always recommend using passages from all religions because this lets us see the one supreme reality from different points of view. Every religion has its own point of view.

There is no disloyalty to your own religion in this. I like the reply that Mother Teresa once gave: "I love all religions, but I am in love with my own."

I'm drawn to the Prayer of Saint Francis, but I have trouble with words like "God" or "Lord" or "divine master."

In meditation, when we repeat the prayer that begins "Lord, make me an instrument of thy peace," we are not referring to anybody outside us. We are calling on our deepest Self, which is the same in all. When I talk about God, I am referring to an underlying reality that is closer to me than this body, dearer to me than my life. In every major religion there is a tradition that maintains, on the basis of direct experience, that this spark of divinity is present in every creature.

Is meditation the same as yoga?

The word *yoga* comes from a root meaning "to unite." In that sense, yoga is that which unites me with the Self, the Lord of Love in my heart. It is both the method and the state of consciousness in which personality is completely united, top to bottom.

When many people use the word *yoga* today, however, they are thinking of the physical exercises called *asanas* in Sanskrit, which are really part of a much larger body of theory and practice that includes meditation. I have benefitted a great deal from these exercises, but if you are practicing the method of meditation I teach, please don't combine it with other methods or with practices that involve controlling the breath or other bodily functions.

Is meditation the same as prayer?
Some of the passages are prayers.

When most people talk about prayer, they mean petitionary prayer: making an appeal for help of some kind from outside. Meditation is very different. Even if the words are those of a prayer, such as the Prayer of Saint Francis, what we are doing with those words in meditation is not asking for anything from outside, but unifying our attention and turning it deep inward to the source of all wisdom within.

In many traditions, this too is called prayer—a deeper kind or "degree" of prayer distinguished by names like "interior prayer" or "prayer of the heart." But whatever the language, we should always remember that in meditation we are not calling on any agency outside us but within, at the very center of our being.

Could you explain more about how you chose the passages in your anthology, *God Makes the Rivers to Flow*?

Some of my criteria are very simple. A meditation passage should be universal, and it must be positive. You may have noticed that in some of the passages I translated for meditation, if there is a negative note in the original it is omitted in my version. These are not just selections for a literary anthology; they are instruments for making very specific changes in personality. When used in meditation, these are living words full of power. You are driving the passages so deep that the contents of mystical awareness they embody will explode like a depth charge, filling your mind and your life with the highest ideals and the skill to translate those ideals into daily behavior. That is why I always insist that the passage be stamped with the personal experience of a man or woman who has realized God. In *God Makes the Rivers to Flow*, in the few cases where the source is in doubt, you can think of these passages as being offered by me directly.

Again, one purpose of a meditation passage is to provide daily inspiration. If it does not stir you inwardly, don't use it at all.

I have been a lover of poetry since childhood, but even beautiful poetry may not be appropriate. Just because a passage is beautiful or dramatic does not mean it is suitable for meditation.

Last — but definitely not least — the passage should be thoroughly practical. It should express values that can be translated into daily living with great benefit to yourself, your family, and your community. This is a quality not easily found. Poetry and practicality need not always go together; profundity and practicality need not always go together. Many scriptures in the great religions do not lend themselves to daily practice. If you ask me, for example, how to get over anger, I can tell you: one, two, three, four. If you ask how to get over greed, I can tell you: one, two, three, four. That's the kind of practice that is essential.

So although we can choose our own passages to meditate on, you recommend that we select them from your anthology? Not from other sources?

When you are following the words with complete concentration, the passage is a powerful instrument for making changes in consciousness of which we are not aware. Not every passage that appeals to you on the surface level will work beneath the surface of consciousness. That is why I ask everyone to choose from the passages in *God Makes the Rivers to Flow,* which I have chosen very carefully from many, many possible selections to ensure that each one will contribute positively to the transformation of character, consciousness, and conduct.

I have been combining passage meditation with another method of meditation. Is it really a problem if I do this?

To borrow the words of Sri Ramakrishna, having more than one teacher or more than one method of meditation is like digging too many wells at the same time. You won't get water anywhere at all.

In meditation, what we are trying to do is slowly unify consciousness. Trying to follow more than one teacher or more than one method is just the opposite of this. Most people will find an initial period of exploration necessary, but the spiritual journey only begins when we select a teacher and resolve to follow his or her method of meditation without reservations.

This is not just a matter of impeding progress. Most of the activity in meditation is below the surface of consciousness, where combining instructions can be combustible without our even being aware of what is happening. To take just one example, there are powerful breathing exercises which are followed in the great monasteries of the Himalayas. Very stringent conditions are applied because such exercises are intended to be practiced in environments where food and air are pure and the mind is completely protected from sensory stimulation. When these conditions are not met, even such seemingly simple disciplines as breathing exercises can damage the nervous system without one even being aware of what is happening. I have seen cases of this myself. That is why I never recommend any kind of breathing exercises to anyone trying to follow my method of meditation.

I find it very hard to meditate for thirty minutes. Can I do fifteen? That seems long enough!

That's a very important question. I tried to work this out when

I began, and I discovered that less than thirty minutes is not enough time. It's like physical exercise. We are supposed to exercise for thirty minutes to get aerobic. My personal observation is that we need thirty minutes of concentrated meditation to get the mental aerobic effect.

I love meditation and really want to go deeper. Can I meditate for longer than thirty minutes?

If you want to meditate more, what I suggest is that you meditate again in the evening. This is a case where more time is not better, and in some cases it can be dangerous.

What takes place in meditation is not just going through the words of the passage slowly. When concentration is deep, all physiological processes can be slowed down, and the pressure may be more than your nervous system can take. Again, this is from personal observation of many, many students. I have seen a few people who, in their enthusiasm, disregarded these instructions and got into serious trouble. There are other dangers too.

If you can meditate for half an hour every morning and evening without fail, at the same time, with sustained enthusiasm, and give your very best to the rest of these disciplines during the rest of every day, your meditation cannot help deepening dramatically. It is not the duration that matters; it is the depth. If you are increasing your concentration and keeping your mind calm and one-pointed during the day, distractions in meditation will become fewer and fewer and your mind will slow down naturally.

In your books you seem to say that meditation can banish depression.

Life today is so fraught with problems that it is natural to feel burdened by them and to doubt one's capacity to deal with them effectively. In such cases, the burden often comes not so much from the problems themselves as from the inability we feel about dealing with them. In such situations, meditation can help decisively by releasing inner resources that are available to all of us but are often hidden by clouds of insecurity and doubt.

Chronic depression, however, is a very different matter. This kind of condition can be life-threatening, and it requires expert attention. In such cases I urge everyone to work closely with a qualified professional, and in particular never to combine this method of meditation with psychoactive drugs. Meditation may seem simple, but we should always remember that we are dealing with the most powerful instrument the world has seen.

Can anyone meditate?

In principle everyone can learn to meditate, but there are practical limitations.

I don't recommend this method for children — say, for anyone younger than eighteen — because a certain measure of experimentation with life is required to learn that nothing outside can satisfy us. If you want to give your children a flying start for when they are ready, I recommend the mantram — and the younger they start, the better.

Even for adults, there are a few who are not in a situation where this method can be practiced safely. As I said, I don't recommend my method of meditation for anyone using psychoactive drugs or living in a controlled environment such as a prison. Other methods may help in such environments, but I can speak only from what I know.

Here too, what I would recommend is the mantram, and only when the instructions in my books are followed very carefully.

I've had some unusual experiences in meditation — strange thoughts and sensations.

Knowing the mind, I can assure you that it has a number of aces up its sleeve. The day you start to meditate seriously, the mind knows it is going to be told to listen to you, and the mind doesn't like that at all. It may do its best to distract you with sensations such as nausea or an overwhelming urge to cough or other, more outrageous phenomena. In such cases, the very best strategy is to give more attention to the inspirational passage. When you give more attention to the words, you will not pay attention to these distractions. That's the answer.

The inspirational passage, let me keep repeating to you, is your safety net. Never let go of the inspirational passage whatever the temptation or the difficulty. Ignore all distracting phenomena and keep your mind on the passage. On a deeper level of consciousness there is a kind of Alice's Wonderland on either side where you cannot distinguish between fancy and fiction. This can be quite harmful, so it is best to be scrupulous about holding on to the passage right from the beginning.

One reason we may find lights and sounds and so on intriguing is that we take them for evidence of progress. Something is happening! Beneath my gentle ways, however, I am a very hard-nosed mystic. I'm not impressed by supernatural experiences;

I look for changes in character and conduct. How selfless can you be? Can you restrain your senses when necessary? Can you go against your self-will when it benefits those around you? How long is your span of attention? These are the signs of progress in meditation.

Could you say more about signs of progress?

First and foremost, you will begin to consider the joy of others a little more important than your own. That will probably begin with your family and friends and then extend to your co-workers, but generally your sense of separateness from those around you will be less and less, so you identify with each of them more easily. And that will rub off on them too.

Secondly, your senses will gradually come more and more under your control. As you begin to look upon your body as a vehicle of loving service, for example, your motivation for eating will become very different.

What about during meditation itself?

I can give you a few little hints as to the signs of absorption. One of the earliest is that your senses slowly close down. You become so completely absorbed in the inspirational passage that there are no sounds, no distractions. As Teresa of Avila says, all the bees of the senses have come back to their hive and are sitting there quietly making honey. Sounds, though there may be a dim awareness of them, will seem at first as if they are coming from far, far away. Eventually you will not be aware of them at all.

Other physical sensations, too, will cease to impinge on your consciousness. All this will be like writing on water; these distractions will not have any effect at all. You enter a stage of what

I can only call quiet intoxication, in which the body feels almost as if it were not there. This is the beginning of the loss of body-consciousness: the burden of the body seems to have been lifted; the weight of the ego has been laid down.

Second, as you get absorbed, you are no longer dealing with distractions or with the problem of sleep in meditation. Where you used to fall asleep, now you've learned that the very wave of sleep that used to overcome you can be ridden down into deeper consciousness just as a surfer does. When you see a wave of sleep coming from the depths of your consciousness, instead of lowering your head and succumbing, you can jump on the wave of sleep and keep awake, concentrated on the inspirational passage. Then you find that you're not on the same old level of awareness; you have changed to a deeper level.

Incidentally, this conquest of sleep doesn't come suddenly or by magic. There is a very difficult phase where at times, in spite of your best intentions, you fall asleep in meditation and are not even aware that you have fallen asleep. The way to break out of that stage is not during meditation only, but during the rest of the day. You go about being alert about your senses, not yielding to their tantalizing call. You look for opportunities to turn your back on self-will and repeat the mantram more; you become more particular about what you do before you fall asleep at night. This kind of vigilance will enable you to break through not only the last stages of the sleeping problem, but many of the other problematic stages as meditation deepens.

Third, the inspirational passage slows down greatly, but the theme is still clear and the connection is still intact. Please make sure, when the inspirational passage slows down like this, that you're able to keep the connection intact! Otherwise, meditation has not slowed down; it has stopped, leaving you in Alice's Wonderland.

This is a very poor attempt at explaining what cannot really be explained, but these are some of the signs that absorption is slowly beginning. But make sure that you don't let go of the inspirational passage, and that during the day you follow all these disciplines with sustained enthusiasm: repetition of the mantram, training the senses, and particularly, opening your awareness to the people around and not letting self-will or selfishness come in the way.

Could you explain more about how we can make progress in meditation and stay safe?

It is essential in these stages not to lose hold of the passage. It is possible to lose the passage and not even know it, so that you think your mind has slowed down when it is simply wandering in the unconscious. The inspirational passage is your safety line. Whatever happens, you must be able to maintain your concentration. You must be able to hold on to the inspirational passage and not let it go even for a second.

This is very important advice for everybody, beginners and experienced students alike. If you fall asleep, you are losing the inspirational passage. If your mind wanders, you are losing the inspirational passage. If your attention is divided, you are losing the inspirational passage. If you are not giving your very best attention, you are losing the inspirational passage. So whatever happens, don't let go of the passage; don't let it slip away. I don't have any hesitation in saying that as long as you can cling continuously to the inspirational passage, you can descend to any depth in the mind in safety.

I've been meditating for some time now, but it seems to be getting more difficult.

The Gita gives very good advice: the only right we have is to do what we can; the results are not in our hands. Don't give up; keep trying and all this will come to fruition. Gandhi says, "Full effort is full victory." That is all you are concerned with. Do everything you can and leave the results in the hands of the Lord.

In the early stages of meditation, most of us are likely to do fairly well. Many, many times — perhaps even hundreds — when I asked students after a few months how their meditation was going, they would say naturally, "Oh, very well. I don't see anything so difficult as you make it out to be." And I learned to be patient and say, "Very good. I am glad; you seem to be a natural." Then, after a few months more, I would ask again, "How is your meditation?" And they would reply, "Stuck."

This is the rhythm of meditation: a little progress, then getting stuck. That's the time when you just keep on plugging. Keep on, keep at it, keep at it, keep at it, until the Lord gives you another push from within and you break through to a deeper level.

All this can be bewildering, and much of it cannot be understood at all until later, when you look back. That is why I keep repeating that whenever meditation is difficult, whenever it is disappointing, whenever it doesn't seem to be going anywhere, don't concern yourself with results; don't ask if you are going forward or backwards or sideways. We have nothing to do with these things; our part is simply to do our best.

I can relate to meditation, but why talk about all the other disciplines in your eight-point program?

All these points help each other. Sense training, for example, is not only necessary for health; it helps the mind be one-pointed, just as a one-pointed mind helps train the senses. Both help govern negative passions, and transforming passions helps to still the mind, which is the goal of meditation.

Putting meditation first makes all the other disciplines easier, which in turn helps take your meditation deeper. Repeating the mantram throughout the day keeps the mind calm and kind when you run into trouble, and being able to go through the day with a calm mind means fewer distractions in meditation. If you do all these with a continuous flow of attention, you will be deepening your meditation and your whole life.

"In other words," one friend complained, "you can't join the union if you don't have a job, and you can't get a job if you're not in the union." In those days I didn't know how to answer that kind of remark, but today I just say, don't look upon these as separate disciplines. They are all ways of doing the same thing: training the mind, quietening the mind. But the foundation is the regular, daily practice of meditation.

How should we deal with the strong emotions that sometimes come up during meditation?

We should never forget that meditation is a superb discipline — and the emphasis is always not on superb, but on discipline.

Even in the early years of meditation, there are many times when waves of emotion can sweep over us. That is the time to concentrate more and not to observe the emotion or analyze it, either during meditation or during the day. Don't try to bask in the emotion or wallow in it. I think it is Catherine of Siena who warns that in such cases we can be like a bee that is caught in its own honey. When you are able to concentrate even more on the passage during a wave of emotion, it becomes a valuable aid. You are able to harness it – not consciously, but because it is absorbed into your concentration. Instead of letting it act as a deterrent, it becomes a valuable factor in your progress.

Even after meditation, some of the backlog of such experiences may follow you into the day. Don't dwell on them, don't describe them to others, don't write about them. Every time that wave of emotion comes up, repeat the mantram.

This sounds like suppressing emotions. Isn't that dangerous?

Meditation does not aim at removing emotions. You can turn every negative emotion into positive. Anger, fear, greed, and other destructive emotions are power that can be transformed and harnessed for going forward. So don't think that you have to get rid of your emotions. What you have got to learn is to be in the driver's seat and not let your emotions drive you.

I want to make a difference in the world, and I worry that spending time in meditation is self-indulgent. Can my practice really help other people and not just myself?

Before I took to meditation I was a very literary type of chap. My world was mostly the world of letters. I was never an unkind man, and I don't think I harmed anybody at all, but most of the time all that I was concerned about was literature. But I had some fleeting awareness of the unity of life, and when I came across suffering it really used to shatter me. It would haunt my dreams. What made it so thoroughly disheartening was my inability to relieve it. I did have a desire to contribute to life; many of us in those days, inspired by Gandhi, wanted to make some contribution to a free India. But I knew I didn't have the capacity.

It was only after I took to meditation that I realized there are resources in each of us that can be of benefit to a lot of people. Meditation on an inspirational passage drives the ideals of that passage deep into consciousness, where tremendous resources are waiting to be brought up to the surface and harnessed in selfless service. The deeper you go, the greater the resources, and with that will come greater opportunities for service.

I have good reason to believe that even one person who meditates can influence everyone around. Even though we may not see it, the ripples of selfless work do spread. I feel I have concrete evidence now that even a few good, energetic, loving people practicing meditation will be able to bring about salutary changes in our country and our society very quietly, without claiming any credit at all.

Actually, if you look at the work of the Blue Mountain Center, you will see it has only one root. I just want to reduce suffering. I want to release people from the great burden of suffering that comes to everyone today, whether rich or poor, by showing everyone how to transform anger into compassion, ill will into good will, and hatred into love. I don't go in for demonstrations, but according to the Buddha, the real activists are those who banish anger and greed and hatred and violence from the human heart.

I've been meditating for some time now and have really noticed the benefits. Could you give us more advice on how to go deeper?

I can make a number of practical suggestions. It does not matter whether you have been meditating for a long time or a short time; all these suggestions are equally applicable.

Surprisingly, it is not during meditation that you make progress in meditation; it is during the rest of the day. What you do in meditation is get the power, install the dynamo; the actual work is done after you open your eyes, get up, and go out into the world.

In the actual practice of meditation, when you are going through an inspirational passage like the Prayer of Saint Francis of Assisi – "Grant that I may not so much seek to be consoled as to console, to be understood as to understand" – you are driving these precious words deeper and deeper into the unconscious. That's what concentration means. If the words fall so deep into the unconscious that they begin to change your ways of thinking and reacting, that is what meditation is for: we become what we meditate on.

But that doesn't happen if you meditate and then spend the rest of the day following the same old patterns, reacting in the same old manner. We need to draw upon the power released in meditation to implement the words on which we are meditating. At the breakfast table, when there is a little provocation, you should be able to smile and come up with a kind word. In the evening, when you come home tired, you should still be able to be kind and supportive. This is how old habits are changed, old patterns of thinking are transformed – with little changes in thought and behavior during the rest of the day.

That is why I say that it's not enough if you meditate regularly. The rest of your day must facilitate that meditation. If you have a good meditation in the morning and then yield to compulsive urges, dwell on yourself, or get self-willed or angry, you are undoing all the work you did that morning in meditation.

On the other hand, if you go on doing your best to follow the rest of this eight-point program throughout the day, not only are you going to have a better meditation on the following day, you are beginning to solve your problems and even to help other people solve theirs. When you're able to do your job with cheerful concentration, when you can give and take when things go wrong, when you're working under pressure and are able to remain kind, you're helping your meditation immensely. So try to remember every day that you are participating in meditation even at breakfast, at work, at school, in the garden, everywhere.

So the calmer we stay during the day, the better our next meditation.

Most people could make a lot more progress in meditation if they would learn to keep the mind from getting agitated. That is one thing I learned quickly, right in the midst of my university work. I had all kinds of responsibilities and difficulties, and often even personal conflicts, and I found quickly that if I could keep from getting agitated when dealing with these problems, I could see the results in meditation the very next morning.

In the Gita, this skill is called *vairagya*: the absence of personal entanglement, in which things and people are valued for what we want to get from them. Don't get entangled in anything, the Gita means: don't get all embroiled in how you feel about it or how you think it will benefit you. Whatever you do, do it with detachment. Gradually you can learn to concentrate completely on the job at hand – whether it is interesting or not, whether it appeals to you or not – and then drop it at will at the end of the day.

This skill is essential for improving meditation, for to the extent you are glued to the events and problems of the day, you can't help taking them home with you. The day's distractions will slip into your mind, where they will continue to claim your attention while you're asleep and insist on more attention the next morning in meditation.

This doesn't mean neglecting your work, of course. Just the opposite: you give whatever you are doing your complete attention, your very best effort; then, when you go home, you give your full attention there too. Full attention everywhere – an unbroken thread of attention throughout the day.

What about working on our relationships? Does that also help our meditation?

The same strategy applies to personal entanglements, which is where almost every human being has trouble. If you want to give your best to any relationship, you have to be detached – not from others, but from yourself. Otherwise you'll always be thinking about what you can get from that relationship. If you're completely detached from yourself, you'll be thinking about what you can give. You come to feel the needs of everybody else exactly as if they were your own, which means you cannot be negative, you cannot be unkind, you can only be supportive.

And this, in turn, helps meditation. You can remind yourself every day that progress depends upon how much you are aware of the needs of others and how much you try to meet those needs. Even though we hear this often, it is not easy to keep it in mind. That is why I say it over and over again: being aware of the needs of all those around you helps your absorption in meditation. The connection is easy to see if you think about the other side of the coin: if you get absorbed in your own private pleasures and profit, that will act as an impediment to this ideal of total absorption.

Remind yourself every day, therefore, to cultivate a sense of proportion, a sense of what truly matters. I hear petty personal differences being ventilated as fundamental issues of life and death — differences so ridiculously small that to waste time and vitality over them is tragic. If you can keep yourself from getting agitated by such things and keep your mind on an even keel throughout the day, taking the rough with the smooth, the Gita would say you are mastering the art of living. If you can laugh it off when things go against you while still giving your very best, you are mastering the art of living. If you are able to throw yourself heart and soul into a selfless job that you don't like, or work harmoniously with difficult people instead of ploughing a lonely furrow, you are mastering the art of living. And all of these skills will take your meditation deeper day by day.

I'm still finding so many distractions coming up in my meditation.

In the early days, when I had to look through mountains of meditation notebooks from my students at Cal, one question that kept coming up was "Why do I have so many distractions in meditation?" I would write, "Because you have so many distractions during the day."

Where do distractions come from? Where do *your* distractions come from? The list may seem different for each person, but the variations are just details. Everyone gets distracted by the same kinds of thoughts: work, family, past experiences to relive or regret, future events to plan for or get anxious about. It's a very familiar catalogue, and the answer is universal: to minimize distractions, go to the source — where they arise.

Minimizing self-will is minimizing distractions. Reducing the number of things one does to please oneself is reducing the number of distractions. The more you starve self-will, the fewer distractions you will have. That is the all-important connection between meditation and the rest of the day.

Here is a good motto to have on your desk, which I think is taken from Sri Aurobindo: "All life is yoga." For the true spiritual aspirant, every day is yoga day. Every moment there is a choice, from the time you wake up until you go to bed: shall I do what is temporarily pleasing, appealing to my ego or senses or self-will — which is very easy for everybody — or shall I choose to do what will benefit all? Shall I eat what appeals to me, or shall I choose food that will strengthen my body to work for all? Shall I refrain from doing trivial little things to please myself so that I can give my time to helping others? There are choices like this all day long — and interestingly enough, as you keep on making right choices, you'll find fewer distractions in your meditation.

Could you tell us what happens when there are no more distractions in meditation? What's it like?

When there are no distractions in meditation, the mind process slows down automatically. And when the mind slows down in meditation, you go deeper into consciousness. These two go hand in hand: in fact, the slow, unbroken flow of attention is what sinking deeper into consciousness means.

Below a certain depth in meditation, when you have really learned to concentrate, there will be a living charge in the words on which you are meditating. Then it's no longer a line that you are reciting; if your concentration is unbroken, the words will fall right into the depths of your consciousness, where they come to life. "When you keep thinking about sense objects, attachment comes . . ." As you are repeating words like these from the Gita, their application also comes along, not just their meaning, bringing with it an appeal – "Don't let your mind dwell on sense objects" – and a kind of resolution not to let your attention wander to sense objects because "attachment breeds desire, the lust of possession which, when thwarted, burns to anger . . ."

Now all the practical applications of those words will come. Such a wealth of application to daily living! You're no longer meditating on words; you are meditating on the vital applications of eternal truths. And the test is that after you finish your meditation, the application of the words will follow you, helping you make the best choices throughout the day. That is the proof that your meditation has been good. If you see that the vital applications of the inspirational passage are with you, your meditation has been very good. If they are not with you, there is still considerable room for improvement.

The secret here is unifying your desires around this supreme goal. Due to the inestimable blessing of my teacher's love, once I turned to meditation, there was nothing that I wanted except awareness of God, and for that I was prepared to pay any price that was asked of me. That very desire, as it grew stronger and stronger, gradually consumed all my smaller desires, so that my progress in meditation was rather rapid—just because I did not have many other desires and distractions to struggle against.

So try to focus your attention all the time on the supreme goal. Renew your commitment every day. It is a commitment that will benefit everyone around you. And as your spiritual awareness grows, you'll find more and more opportunities for contributing to the welfare of those around you. Remind yourself every day that meditation is not for your benefit alone; it is for the benefit of the whole world.

The Mantram

**Is there a difference between "mantram" and "mantra,"
as it is usually spelled?**

They are the same word. *Mantram* is the neuter form, and that
is the traditional way that kind of noun has been taught in India
for thousands of years. In modern linguistics, the form used is
masculine, *mantra*. There is no difference at all, but since *mantra*
has become so common in phrases like "the Wall Street mantra,"
I prefer to keep to the form I learned as a child.

**You say that we should choose our own mantram,
but that it should be one from your recommended list.
Could you explain why that is?**

Usually we receive the mantram from our teacher. In many of
the Indian traditions, this is a secret between the teacher and
the student. You are not supposed to tell anyone what your mantram is. Some people respond to that, and I have no quarrel with
it whatever. But I belong to another tradition, which I call the
tradition of the open hand: I say, "These are the great mantrams;
you choose." I like the intelligent cooperation of the student, and

I try to help those who come to me to make a wise choice. The mantram still comes from me, but you can make your own choice.

In choosing, however, please don't go by whether it sounds nice or it "feels right." That is not the issue. Has it been honored by time, practiced by millions? Does your teacher give it? There are certain requirements for a mantram of which most people are not aware. That is why I limit the mantrams in my books to a very few chosen ones that can always be trusted because they are universal, applicable to all countries and to all people. They come to us already surcharged with energy.

Is that why we shouldn't make up our own mantram?

The mantram should carry the power of many centuries of people who have used the mantram and benefitted by it. That is how the mantram becomes holy. *Rama,* for example, has been used as a mantram for thousands of years. The name of Jesus has been repeated as a mantram and hallowed by millions of Christians down the centuries. A mantram draws its power from the long procession of religious people who have used it. That's why when you make up your own mantram, it has no power: the power comes from the source.

Most important, you should receive the mantram "hot," from someone who has verified it in his or her personal experience. My own mantram — *Hare Rama, Hare Krishna* — is important for me not only because it has been used for thousands of years in India, but because I received it scalding hot from my own teacher, my grandmother — so hot that I cannot hold it at all; I've got to pass it on to everybody.

What do you mean by someone "verifying" a mantram?

The mantram should bear the imprint of the spiritual awareness of the person giving it – someone who has brought it to life in his or her own consciousness. The stamp of this experience shows in everything they say and do. The great mystics whose history has come down to us tell us they have seen Rama, the reality indicated by the mantram, in the depths of consciousness. They have seen Krishna, the reality indicated by the mantram. They have seen Jesus, indicated by the Jesus Prayer. These are direct experiences of the same reality.

Can I make up a mantram from holy words? Wouldn't that have the same power?

Quite a number of people ask me this. They say, "I have made up this mantram; what do you think of it? 'I love God, I love God, I love God.'" Well, pretty good statement, but not quite a mantram. I usually say, "Are you an illumined person?" That is the first qualification. Second, "How many millions of devotees have used your mantram?" And third, "Is there anyone who has verified this mantram in the depths of consciousness?" These are the important criteria in the choice of the mantram, which is why I recommend mantrams that are stamped with the spiritual awareness of the world's great teachers.

Some of the mantrams you recommend don't seem to come from a tradition. For example, Saint Francis wouldn't have used the words "My God and my all." Wouldn't he have been praying in Italian?

I believe he actually used Church Latin: *Deus meus et omnia,* which is a beautiful mantram that I understand has also been sanctified in other languages, including English, by centuries of repetition by devoted Franciscans around the world. If you like, however, you may regard all the mantrams I recommend as coming from me. You are still getting them hot.

The mantrams that you recommend all sound religious, and I'm not religious. What should I do?

Many people today are averse to the religion of their childhood or to organized religion in any form at all. As I understand it, religion is beyond sectarian divisions and dogmas. It is realization of the unity of life. That supreme reality is what all mantrams stand for. All mantrams lead to that reality, and all have come down to us from men and women who have made that discovery themselves. To follow in their footsteps, there is no need for us to believe in anything; we have simply to trust them enough to make the experiment ourselves.

Isn't *Om* a great mantram? Can I just say *Om*?

Om – or, as it is sometimes spelled, *Aum* – is not really a word, not even a sound in the usual sense. It stands for a primordial vibration which can be experienced in very deep meditation, to which all mantrams lead.

So if you look at some of the great mantrams that have come down to us in India – for example, *Om nama Shivaya,* or *Om Yesu Christu* – you will see that *Om* has been added to one of the names of God or a great incarnation. If you want to use *Om,* that is what I would recommend – but always make sure it is a traditional mantram sanctified by centuries of tradition.

Are any of the mantrams on your list more effective than the others? I'm worried I might not choose the one that's right for me.

Generally speaking, if a mantram comes out of a holy tradition, I think it is a good choice. All mantrams will take you to the final goal, as you can experience for yourself. When you have verified the *Rama* mantram, for example, you know that all mantrams are the same.

I once met a man from Harvard who had spent about twelve years in an Indian ashram under a Hindu teacher with a Sanskrit mantram. When he finally had the supreme vision, he told us, it was of Jesus the Christ. He couldn't get over it. I said, "It is all the same; only the costume is different." When you finally see the Self, it doesn't matter what religion you belong to, or whether you belong to any religion at all. The Self has no religion. The Self has no color. The Self has no caste. How you experience the supreme reality depends upon your innermost need. Whether you call on Krishna or Rama or Jesus the Christ, or use the Buddhist mantram *Om mani padme hum,* when the supreme revelation comes, you'll find it is "*Ramakrishnajesusbuddha,*" one divine reality that has all kinds of names.

Can you have the same mantram as your spiritual teacher?

Yes. In fact, if you have a teacher, it's traditional to choose your teacher's mantram. But there is actually no obligation to have your teacher's mantram. If you choose a traditional mantram like *Rama, Rama* or the Jesus Prayer or *Om mani padme hum,* it is already surcharged—"batteries included."

I appreciate meditation, but the mantram seems so irrational.

The practical answer is just to try it and see for yourself. So far as I know, we still don't really understand how aspirin works, yet we have faith in aspirin. When you take the bottle off the bathroom shelf and pop a couple of pills into your mouth, you are saying in effect, "I believe. I have faith that this will work." I would say, "Take plenty of mantrams too." It is equally good advice: one for fever in the body, the other for the fever of self-will.

People sometimes retort, "We don't think it will work." I reply, "Don't you think you can give the Buddha or Jesus the Christ as much credence as you give Mr. Bayer?" That is all I am asking for. There is nothing wrong if we start repeating it a little skeptically, but we can treat it as an experiment that each one of us has to conduct for ourselves.

Isn't it just mindless repetition?

In the early days, when I was more candid, I would say that "mindless repetition" is often what we are pleased to call thinking. The mind just runs along on its own, repeating whatever comes to it. The mantram is mindful repetition — and repetition is really the whole point, because you are trying to fill in the gaps in consciousness so that this mindless flow of disjointed thoughts cannot take over.

Repeating the mantram is like walking from one place to another: say, from San Francisco to New York, about three thousand miles. You don't expect to do that without repetition, one step after the next, in order to reach your goal. Repeating the mantram, too, is a journey.

Similarly, the mantram has been called a ladder with billions and billions of steps, rising from earth to heaven. It's sheer repetition, limitless repetition, but with each repetition you are going somewhere. You are quietening the mind.

When people come to me with a problem that they can't get out of their minds and ask, "What can I do?" I say, "Just repeat the holy name." You can find occasion to repeat it a thousand times every day, ten thousand times every day.

Can we also write the mantram if we're struggling with a problem?

When Christine and I visited Swami Ramdas's ashram in India, we saw how he used writing the mantram in this way. He did not encourage people to talk because he thought most talk about personal problems does not serve any useful purpose. Instead he had a pile of what in India are called exercise books: blank notebooks with lots and lots of pages. When somebody would come to Swami Ramdas with a load of problems, Ramdas would say, "Here is an eighty-page exercise book. You just write *Rama, Rama, Rama, Rama,* fill it up, and bring it to me." It takes a lot of mantrams to fill up an eighty-page exercise book. By the time the person had filled it up, he would come back to Ramdas calmer and more compassionate. That is the whole point, you see: Problems bother us because they agitate the mind. The problem is not the problem; it is the agitation. And the work of the mantram is to quieten the agitation in the mind.

How did you fit in those thousands of repetitions?
I don't have the time.

This is what I hear from everybody. I comfort them by saying that's what I used to tell myself. In the early days, I too used to think I didn't have time for repeating the mantram. I was always active, as I still am. I had many, many vital interests, and what little time I had I would give to my students.

But when I began to long for the state where the mantram will begin to repeat itself, I longed for it so much that I worked for it at every possible opportunity. Standing in a queue, riding in a car, walking to the next classroom, waiting at the post office, before a meal, going to sleep – as the bank advertisement says, it all adds up.

But you need to look for opportunities. Many of the occasions when we get bored, for example, it is simply because we don't know how to use the time. Often we make silly statements, indulge in gossip, do silly things, or offend people with thoughtless words. All this could be saved just by repeating the mantram.

Can I sing the mantram? Chant it? Say it aloud?

If you are alone, you can repeat the mantram aloud to yourself, especially to get it started if you are agitated. If you are with other people, however, repeating it audibly can be confusing – and if they happen to have a mantram of their own, they are likely to be trying to repeat it themselves. The mantram is always most effective when repeated in the mind.

In India, as you know, devotional people like to come together to sing songs about the glory of God composed by some of our great mystics. But this is more a spiritual exercise than a musical exercise. It is possible for anyone to sing the mantram beautifully, but that is not its purpose. It is far more important to pay attention to the devotional part of it than the musical part. I remember Mahatma Gandhi, commenting on a distinguished singer in India, saying that there is always a possibility that you may get so absorbed in the music that you forget the devotional aspect of it. There may even come a time when the musical part becomes an impediment on the spiritual path: you may get so attached to the sensual pleasure that you stop there.

Here what I encourage is that we repeat the mantram silently in the mind and meditate deeply. If you like, you can always sing the mantram in your mind.

How can I encourage my children to use the mantram? And which mantram should I give to them?

The repetition of the mantram is a very valuable tool for all children everywhere. It can be used while going to the dentist. It can be used during examination time. It can be used at school. It can be used while competing in school.

You can introduce it through the life of Mahatma Gandhi. Explain how great a blessing he has been to the world and then, when they ask you "How did he become like that?" you talk about the power of the mantram.

There is no mantram better for children than Gandhi's mantram, *Rama,* but you can also suggest your own mantram if it has been chosen from my list. It can be a great benefit when all members of the family use the same mantram.

How early should we introduce our children to the mantram? When did you start?

If you want to know when my spiritual life started, personally I started halfway through life, but today I would say that my spiritual life really began in my mother's womb when she was repeating her mantram given by her mother, who was God-conscious, repeating it all the time, so I got the full benefit of it.

In most religious homes in India the training of the baby starts with the mother when she's pregnant. Just as nourishing food taken by the mother strengthens the baby, nourishing mantrams repeated by the mother strengthen the baby. One is strengthening the body, the other is strengthening the mind.

How can we use the mantram with young children? Where should we start?

For the little ones, when they are crying, you can sing the mantram. That's the best lullaby, and this is how you let the mantram get deeper into the mind of the child even before he or she is aware. That is how I received the power of the mantram from my grandmother, without even knowing that I was receiving it.

Teach your child to repeat the mantram at night. Many of my friends sing the mantram to their children as a lullaby; it is more important than bedtime storytelling. Let Humpty Dumpty fall, let Jack and Jill go up the hill; the mantram can't wait. It will remove fears from your child's heart; it will refresh your child's sleep.

Similarly, whenever your child is afraid or angry, just teach him or her to repeat the mantram. And the very best way to teach a child anything is for the father and mother to practice it themselves. The mantram may take a while to catch on, but it will give your children armor that the forces of life cannot break.

Can I meditate on the mantram? Isn't that done in India?

Not only in India, but in other mystical traditions too, the mantram is used for meditation. In my presentation, however, I draw a distinction between meditation on an inspirational passage and repetition of the mantram. To meditate on an inspirational passage, you need to be seated with your concentration focused on the words of the passage. But the mantram you can repeat at any time that concentration is not required.

How do meditation and the mantram work together in your program?

Both these disciplines help each other. The more you repeat your mantram, the deeper will be your meditation. The deeper your meditation, the better will be your repetition of the mantram. That is why, in my presentation, meditation and the mantram go together.

In addition, when you are meditating in the morning and again in the evening, repetition of the mantram helps as a kind of connecting thread, using the odd moments of the day.

Of course, this requires taking advantage of every opportunity. I learned to meditate at a great university in India where I had grave responsibilities and a very tight schedule. I learned to pick up every minute like a miser picking up a dime. If I got just two minutes, I would walk and repeat the mantram. And I seldom took part in unnecessary talk; instead I would go sit in a corner, close my eyes, and repeat the mantram. My colleagues thought I was catching forty winks; I was catching forty mantrams.

The reward for all that persistent effort — this is the miracle of my teacher's blessing — is that today I don't have to repeat the mantram. It repeats itself. And when the mantram repeats itself, no negative thought can come in; no wave of anger can enter the mind. That is what everyone should aim at.

Can we attain this advanced spiritual state just by systematic repetition of the mantram? Do we really need meditation as well?

To be established in the mantram is self-realization. It is nirvana. In today's world, for the vast majority of ordinary people like us who have so much self-will and have been so thoroughly conditioned by the mass media, I don't think it is possible to reach this state through repetition of the mantram alone. Even though I was brought up in a good Hindu household at the feet of my spiritual teacher, I didn't have the kind of utter surrender in love to the Lord that is necessary for becoming established in the mantram. That is why I say, based on my own experience, that the regular, sincere, systematic practice of meditation is required.

First and foremost, therefore, please be regular about your meditation. Please be sincere about your practice and make the very best effort in it. Then use every opportunity you have for repeating the mantram.

Why is walking with the mantram so important?

Rhythmic physical activity helps greatly to get the mantram going and keep it going deeper and deeper, which is especially necessary when dealing with powerful emotions. The rhythm of the mantram combines with the rhythms of a hard, fast walk to steady the rhythms of breathing and thinking, transforming the emotion from negative into positive.

Can you give practical examples of when you would do this?

Whenever there are differences at the office, differences at the workplace or at home, that is the best time for repeating the mantram because then you have more power. The negative emotion can always be used as a heavy hammer to drive the mantram in.

When you are angry, when you are resentful, when you are afraid, when you are greedy, when you are frustrated, please go for a long, fast walk — outside if you can; if necessary, around the block; if you can't even go around the block, walk in the lobby or up and down the stairs. Our bank in Berkeley had a long lobby where one could walk. Most shopping malls are ideal. You will gradually find that a negative emotion gives more power to the repetition of your mantram. Instead of taking away from your peace of mind, it gives you more peace of mind. Instead of adding to your difficulties, it helps to solve them.

When you talk about walking fast and timing the mantram with your stride and your breathing, do you literally mean we should say it fast?

No, no, don't say it fast. Say it in rhythm: *Ra-ma, Ra-ma, Ra-ma,* not *Ramramramrammmmma.*

But if we repeat the mantram while walking, isn't that being two-pointed?

The intellect loves questions like this, but they tend to fall away when you actually try the mantram. Then you see for yourself that once the mantram catches on, the mind is in focus everywhere.

When walking with the mantram, for example, the mantram actually makes you more wakeful, more alert to what is going on around you. It will heighten your awareness of beauty. Without a mantram, what usually happens is that we get caught listening to our own thoughts, which is never beneficial.

What about when we're with someone? Shouldn't we give the other person our one-pointed attention, even in a difficult conversation? How does the mantram work in these situations?

In listening, it is always best to give the other person your full attention. If the conversation provokes so much agitation that this becomes impossible, however, you can always repeat the mantram to quieten the mind down.

A calm mind can listen with some detachment; an agitated mind often isn't really able to listen at all. The words go in one ear and out the other with no effect in between except to make the mind more agitated. At such times you can repeat the mantram until your mind calms down enough to give one-pointed attention again.

Of course, both these skills — calming the mind with the mantram and giving full attention — will be infinitely easier if you are practicing them at every opportunity during the rest of the day.

When I'm driving on long stretches of road with little traffic, my mind starts to wander because it has nothing to think about. At such times, can I repeat the mantram?

Wherever your attention is required, whether it is driving a car, cutting vegetables, or operating power tools, I wouldn't repeat the mantram, nor would I suggest that you repeat the mantram. Give your concentrated attention to driving. Otherwise you're not only risking your life, you're risking the lives of others.

Once somebody persuaded me to allow her to repeat the mantram on those long Kansas turnpikes where nothing seems to happen for miles. But I had to retract that statement after seeing how people drive.

On a long, empty road, nothing seems to happen until suddenly something does – and then, at sixty miles an hour, a split second of inattention is all that is required to cause a terrible accident. Not long ago, very near where we live, two cyclists were killed by a driver who had been taking for granted a long stretch of apparently empty road.

How about when you're locked in a traffic jam and you aren't going anywhere. Is it all right to say the mantram then?

I used to say that sitting in traffic is a great time for repeating the mantram because you need to stay patient and focused. But even in such circumstances, as a passenger, I have noticed so many unexpected things: a cyclist coming up between vehicles out of nowhere, for example, or a stopped car lurching forward when the driver lets up on a tired foot. Today I say that whatever the situation, being in traffic always requires full attention. This goes for cyclists as well as drivers.

I have been repeating the mantram for some time and it still feels mechanical. It just doesn't seem to work.

You may not be the best judge. In my experience, when someone says a mantram is not working, it usually means that the person using it has not been working.

I used to get this question often in the early days. I would reply, "The mantram works. It will work for you if you do more work yourself." The more you put into it, the greater the benefit you will receive.

For example, when unwanted desires come – as they will to all of us – people sometimes ask why the mantram doesn't keep those thoughts out the way I describe. The answer is that the mantram is just sitting on the couch and saying quietly, "Please go away." Who hears? The mantram should leap to its feet and get to the door before the distraction can even knock. It doesn't need to be violent. It's very gentle, but it is very persistent. It simply blocks the entrance and sends the distracting thought on its way. But for that to happen, we have to get the mantram off the couch.

How can we get established in the mantram in the way you describe?

Ramdas advises, "Have the mantram constantly in your mind." That is the first and last instruction where japam or repetition of the mantram is concerned.

Make use of every spare moment to repeat your mantram. A million opportunities can be discovered during the course of a single day, and of course when you are falling asleep at night.

There may come a time when you cannot sleep and find it almost impossible to go on repeating the holy name hour after hour. The mind gets tired. At such times, I used to ask Sri Krishna in my heart to make it a joy for me to recite his name. As a result, now it is not a discipline; I do it with all the joy of indiscipline. I have no limits now, no restraints. I do it all the time, which is what going beyond all disciplines means. But you have to struggle with disciplines for a long, long time before this kind of spiritual freedom comes.

In my own practice, for example, I found that gradually – over a long, long period, not immediately – the period of japam will go on increasing, particularly when deepening meditation means you don't need so much sleep at night, so that you lie awake resting your body in bed and resting your mind through japam.

Gradually, those hours of conscious sovereignty over the mind will bring increasing freedom in your thoughts and feelings, in your very life. That's the motivation for repeating the mantram.

When a powerful emotion like anger is sweeping me away, what should I do?

If you can, it is very helpful to go out for a fast walk around the block or up and down the hall, repeating the mantram to yourself the whole way. Once your mind has quieted down, you can reflect with some detachment on how painful the long-term consequences of our anger are likely to be for everyone, including yourself. That's a kind of first aid.

But it is helpful to remember that of itself, a strong urge is not something negative. It is power rising, which the mantram can transform for positive use. Anger is one of the most destructive emotions on earth, but the mantram can turn even this fearful power into compassion, as we can see in the life of Mahatma Gandhi.

So a fast walk repeating the mantram can help us to transform anger?

Walking fast with the mantram is always helpful, but how to effect this transformation over the long run depends upon the person and particularly upon the age group. If you are young, for example, I would suggest not just going for a fast walk but going up a long slope repeating the mantram. That's the principle behind pilgrims in India climbing the Himalayas.

For those who are not capable of these physical exploits, I would suggest trying longer walks — two or three hours repeating the mantram. There have been many occasions when I have walked for three to four hours. It's really like a championship match. When a tremendously strong passion like anger has picked you up, in the first bout you won't make any impression at all. You feel like going back to your corner and not coming out again. But if you can keep walking repeating the mantram every time the tidal wave of anger picks you up, after two or three or four hours you can see that you are the master of the situation. Then you see that this tremendous impulse was the offer of additional power to you. It is that aspect I would emphasize. Look upon these bouts as potential power crying out, "Harness me!"

Can we use the mantram to prevent the agitation in the first place?

It is not so much preventing as minimizing the movement of the mind. Encased as we are in a physical body, it is not possible for many of us to completely still the mind in the face of provocation. In most people, when there is agitation, the mind moves back and forth, up and down, like a hammock. It goes on swinging, and we rather enjoy that swinging in a negative way. When we practice meditation, repeat the mantram, and observe the allied disciplines, what happens is that the hammock swings less and less. After a lot of practice, we arrive at the state where, if someone does or says something unkind, there is only a slight swinging of the mind and we are able to stabilize it. But we should always expect a little movement.

When I'm upset I find it really hard to keep the mantram going, and I can't always leave the office, for instance, for a fast walk. Do you have any other suggestions?

Keep a notebook at home and at work, and if you find your mind getting agitated, keep writing the mantram with concentration for one or two pages. You will find that the manual activity helps to focus and steady your mind.

Can I give my mantram to family members and friends? I'd so like them to feel the benefit.

I follow the example of a great South Indian mystic, Ramanuja, whose teacher told him, "Don't reveal your mantram to anybody. They will gain the benefit, but you will lose it all." Ramanuja went straight to the temple tower and called, "Listen to me, everybody who can hear! I want all of you to be happy, even if it means I will be miserable all my life." Of course, his teacher was highly pleased. So share your mantram with anybody who asks for it; I will take the responsibility.

I get caught up in things during the day and forget all about the mantram. How can I help remember it more often?

One thing many people find helpful is to put little reminders where you will see them. I have friends who keep flash cards with them as reminders. But one of the best ways is simply to keep using the mantram as much as you can.

When I began using the mantram, I felt a very strong connection with it. But as time has gone on, it's harder and harder to use it.

The mantram can't help working if you go on repeating it faithfully. Don't wait until you feel upset to use it. You can repeat the mantram anytime, and the more you repeat it, even if you feel it's not working, the more likely it will be there when you need to draw on it in a crisis.

It is amazing how many opportunities you can find during the day, no matter how busy you may be. You may find it helpful to keep a notebook in your room or at your place of work, so you can write the mantram whenever you get a minute or two. If you commute, use the time for the mantram. Irritation, exasperation, frustration, boredom, the desire to keep the tongue moving, are all hammers you can use to drive the mantram deep into the mind, so it can work and heal in the depths of the unconscious.

You said the mantram can help us when we're in pain. Could you say more about that?

I find the mantram helpful everywhere, even in mundane trials. My dentist and dental assistant think I am a stoic, but they are wrong; I simply know how to use my mantram. I am quite sensitive to pain, but as soon as I get into the dental chair I say, "Don't try to tell me who won the baseball game or who is going to get an Academy Award. Just turn the music off and let me repeat my mantram."

I close my eyes and start to repeat *Rama, Rama, Rama,* and within minutes my attention is absorbed. It is not that the drill no longer hurts, but there is no fear of it in my mind; and it is fear that makes pain hard to bear. When fear of pain goes, suffering becomes manageable. And that is what the mantram can do. Whether it is a headache, a stomachache, or serious injury, the mantram always helps.

I want to add that I am not against any reasonable painkiller in the hands of a skilled physician, but whether you have chemical aid or not, repeat the mantram. Not only will it help you manage pain yourself, but the experience will drive the mantram deeper into your consciousness. The next time you need it, the mantram will work from an even deeper level.

Why does the Bhagavad Gita call the mantram a purifier?

Meditation helps the mantram, and the mantram helps meditation. Both work together in the mind to resolve old conditioning so that we can shape our consciousness around a new ideal of our own choosing. That is what purification means. In practice, it means simply the reduction of self-will, a large part of which is simply dwelling on oneself to the exclusion of those around us.

This is very much an internal process. For the transformation of consciousness to be complete, we have to put these new ideals into practice in daily living. So it is very important, right from the beginning, to give your very best not only to meditation, but to the repetition of the mantram and all the other disciplines which apply the power of meditation to daily living.

If, after your meditation, you go off to dwell on yourself and try to avoid people or challenges around you, your consciousness may have been elevated a little in your morning meditation, but it will take the shape of loneliness and separateness during the rest of the day. This is the time to repeat the mantram and be with people, to keep your senses and mind from wandering, to work harmoniously with others and give your complete concentration to the job at hand. In all these ways you are keeping consciousness from reassuming its old, painfully rigid forms.

Once I went for a swim at the home of a friend who had an Olympic-sized pool. Floating around in this pool was some kind of gadget that I couldn't quite figure out, so I asked my host, "What is that for?"

He said, "That's a pool sweep. It keeps on chugging around, removing impurities from the pool wherever it finds them."

I couldn't help teasing him: "You're very careful about keeping this pool clean and pure, but wouldn't you like to purify the pool inside, too?"

He looked blank. I used his language: "*Rama* is an effective pool sweep for the mind; it can float about and remove impurities wherever it finds them, twenty-four hours a day."

So whenever you have a tendency to think about yourself — how much you can get, how much you can grab, or how unfairly life is treating you — don't talk about it, don't analyze it; go for a walk repeating the mantram. This is one of the easiest methods of dealing with thinking about yourself. You will gradually find that the mantram will slowly reduce the level of self-will. After many years, the mantram combined with meditation will bring the mind to a stillness. When the mind is still, there is no self-will. When there is no self-will, the mind is still.

Is it all right to repeat my mantram for other people? Does it help them?

When you get established in your mantram, according to our saints, you can even allocate your japam to a person in need. It's a wonderful gift usually possessed by saints, but all of us can aim at that. When somebody close to you is in need, you can say to yourself, "I'm repeating this mantram for that person's benefit."

It is a kind of repetition of the mantram by proxy. The person is not able to do it, so you are doing it for them. In that way you can allocate your repetition of the mantram to that person, not only when you are with that person but at other times also.

I have a close friend who is dying. Can I use my mantram to help her?

People who are seriously ill, perhaps in their last days, can benefit from the mantram greatly. If they cannot repeat it, hold their hand and keep repeating your mantram silently for them. Some part of your awareness will reach them. You will see for yourself how comforted they will become because of the depth from which you are able to repeat the holy name.

There is no need to talk at such times. Just being together and repeating the mantram, especially if the person is responsive to us, can help a great deal to calm the turbulence that overtakes the mind at the onset of death.

What occupies our consciousness at the moment of death is of the utmost importance. That is why in India some great scripture like the Bhagavad Gita is usually read aloud while a person is dying, so that something of its message will be with that person in his final moments.

Very much the same thing is done in other great religions. Even more effective in this critical transition is for the dying person to repeat the mantram over and over in the mind. The mantram is always a powerful ally, and if we can cling to it at the time of death, we will already have focused a good deal of our consciousness on the Lord.

I have complete confidence that the Lord will always come to my rescue when I call on him from the depths of my heart. That is why I recommend the mantram with such certitude, because I know without doubt it can be relied upon in times of distress. This is the advice many great mystics have given us: to call upon the Lord, by whatever name we use, to help us overcome our enemy, death.

What can we do now to prepare for the time when we are dying?

If we begin now to repeat the mantram, and repeat it whenever we get an opportunity, it will be there when we need it even in the turmoil of the body's final hours. According to Swami Ramdas, when you go on repeating the mantram that your teacher has given you, you'll feel the presence of the teacher always with you. That's why the mantram is said to be the bond between the teacher and the student. When you become established in your mantram, the mantram is your real guru, because the mantram is God.

Even though our repetition may seem mechanical to begin with, if we practice meditation earnestly and support our meditation with a program of spiritual living, the mantram will enable us to go deeper and deeper into our consciousness. Practice is the important thing, and sustained enthusiasm.

Life is so short, and this discovery so urgent and so arduous, that none of us can afford to waste a day in not doing our best to move closer to the goal. Please take advantage of every opportunity to repeat the mantram, to train your senses, to keep on transforming your passions.

And please be regular about your meditation. Don't lose a single day; don't waste a moment doing selfish things. All this time can be utilized for discovering the Self and going beyond death here on this earth.

Other Points

SLOWING DOWN

I worry that if I slow down, I won't get as much done.

Slowing down and one-pointed attention work together. Going slow doesn't mean achieving little. If your concentration is one-pointed, going slow means achieving much. It is essential in this connection not to confuse slowness with sloth, which breeds procrastination and general inefficiency. In slowing down, attend meticulously to details, giving the very best you are capable of even to the smallest undertaking.

Somehow, in our modern civilization, we have acquired the idea that the mind is working best when it runs at top speed. Yet a racing mind lacks time even to finish a thought, let alone to check on its quality. When we slow down the mind, we work better at everything we do. Not only is the quality of our work better, we are actually able to get more done.

I'm still not sure I see the point of this. Why do you attach so much importance to slowing down?

Even to see life, we need to go slow. To enjoy life, we need to go slow. To understand people, to understand situations, to arrive at considered conclusions and to make wise decisions – for all of these, we need time. And this is just what is impossible in a speeded-up civilization; there is no time for anything.

Could you explain more about the link between speed and stress?

Virtually all psychological stress, I would say, comes from the rush and hurry of a frantic mind, which jumps recklessly to unwarranted conclusions, rushes to judgments, and often is going too fast to see events and people as they truly are. Such a mind keeps the body under continual tension. It is constantly on the move, desiring, worrying, hoping, fearing, planning, defending, rehearsing, criticizing; it cannot stop or rest except in deep sleep, when the whole body, particularly the nervous system, heaves a sigh of great relief and tries to repair the damage of the day.

Simply by slowing down the mind – the first purpose of meditation – much of this tension can be removed. Then we are free to respond to life's difficulties not as sources of stress but as challenges, which will draw out of us deeper resources than we ever suspected we had.

Could you say more about the effects of speed on our society today?

I believe it was the historian and philosopher Will Durant who said that any person in a hurry is not civilized. This is not a superficial quip but a profound statement that calls into question the achievements of our technological society. Even though we have attained a level of material abundance that would astonish our ancestors, we seem to have less and less time for what really matters: strengthening the bonds of love that sustain a civilization.

Loving companionship with family members and friends, service to the wider world, periods of reflection on the timeless truths that sustain life — these have been crowded out by a dizzying round of scheduled activities that confer little lasting benefit on anyone.

We are familiar with the concept of famine for food. But there is also famine for time. I don't think we are quite aware of the extent to which we are slowly starving. I would suspect that our sense of time-famine comes from a mind that is speeded up, too distracted to make wise choices between what brings only temporary satisfaction and what is of lasting value. When we complain that there is not enough time, what we really mean is that there is not enough time to do everything we want.

So we try to fit more and more into the same twenty-four-hour period by moving faster or by multitasking — that odd term used by efficiency experts to describe the practice of doing several things at the same time. What starts out as a set of physical habits gradually invades the nervous system. Eventually, a speeded-up life creates a chronically speeded-up mind, and we become incapable of benefiting from the opportunities for leisure and reflection that might come our way. Doing more and more satisfies us less and less. We feel increasingly cut off from what is best in ourselves and from those we want to love.

During nearly forty years as a teacher of meditation in this country, I am glad to say that I have helped thousands of harried men and women slow down and start living richly textured, creative, selfless lives full of meaning and purpose.

Based on this long experience, I would venture to say that the mark of an educated person is the use of time which he or she makes. I think it should be possible to look at a person for a day and make a good guess at how civilized that person is.

What about our children?

It has been a sad observation for me over the past forty years to see that we seem to be passing on to our children our inability to slow down, reflect, and make the wise choices that enrich our own lives and the lives of those around us.

I am not in favor of shunting children from activity to activity, which robs them of their innocence. I see with my own eyes how children are rushed from karate to soccer to gymnastics to ballroom dancing. As beneficial as this training might seem, we need to ask ourselves what is lost when the fleeting years of childhood offer so little chance for looking at the sky, watching the plants and the animals, examining leaves floating in puddles or ants parading along a twig.

Slowing down is closely connected with one-pointed attention: doing one thing at a time, and doing it with complete attention. In the case of rushing, the problem is not only one of speed. Our attention is riveted on ourselves — our needs, our deadlines, our desires — so there is no attention to give to those around us. Especially for children we need to slow down so that we can give them our attention, which they require as much as food and sleep.

How does slowing down fit into the rest of your eight-point program?

When I present the spiritual life, what I am presenting is life at its best — physically, mentally, intellectually, and of course spiritually. It is a total approach based on the practice of meditation, and supported by other allied disciplines which give us the opportunity of living a long, healthy, happy, productive life of selfless service. Each point in my eight-point program of meditation is linked to all the rest. For example, if you slow down, it will help you in making your mind one-pointed, in getting some measure of control over your senses, and in being very supportive of those around you.

In particular, I think everyone today needs to work hard at slowing down, because the pace of life has sped out of control. Every one of us can benefit by planning our day well and going through our tasks with concentration at a slow, even pace which does not put us under undue pressure.

But it's not just about moving physically at a slower pace — it's about slowing down inside?

A hurried pace originates in the mind. You might stop at someone's desk to be sociable, but that doesn't mean your thoughts have stopped. If you're pretending to chat while your mind has sprinted ahead toward the conference room, you might as well take the rest of you there too.

This is the real crux of slowing down: beginning to slow down internally, in the mind. The more we slow down the thinking process, the more control we have over our lives.

Could you explain more about the relationship between a speeded-up mind and negative emotions?

Fear, anger, selfish desire, envy: all these are associated with a speeded-up mind, and when the mind speeds up, it takes basic physiological processes with it. The thinking process hurtles along, thoughts stumble over one another in an incoherent rush— and, on cue, the heart begins to race and breathing becomes quicker, shallow, and ragged.

Interestingly enough, the reverse is also true. Once the mind gets conditioned to speed, not only do speeding thoughts make the body go faster, speeded-up behavior can induce negative emotions as well.

Suppose you've slept through the alarm and are in a rush to get off to work. You rip through the kitchen like a whirlwind, grabbing whatever you need as you go, trying to button your shirt while you eat your toast on your way out the door. The next time you catch yourself like this, watch and see how prone your mind is to negative responses.

Everything seems an obstruction or a threat. Your children look hostile — if you see them at all — and even the dog seems out to ruin your day, draping herself right across the threshold in the hope of tripping you up. "Watch out!" the kids say once you're gone. "It's going to be another of those mean-mood days."

A thrilling realization comes when you begin to understand this two-way relationship between speeded-up thinking and negative emotions. If you are chronically angry, fearful, or greedy, you know well how much damage these tendencies have done to your relationships. And you know, too, how dauntingly hard they are to change when you approach them head-on. Their roots go deep in your past conditioning. You can talk them out, analyze them in your dreams, reason with yourself, go to anger workshops and fear seminars; still they wreak havoc, out of control.

How does meditation help us to slow down?

Suppose that instead of going after chronic anger or fear directly, you were to tackle the thought process itself – the mind in its Indianapolis speedway mode. When a car is going a hundred miles per hour, you can't safely slam on the brakes. But you can lift your foot off the accelerator. From one hundred miles per hour the speed drops to ninety-eight, then to ninety-five, then ninety, until finally you're cruising along at a safe and sane fifty-five. You've decelerated gradually and safely.

This is exactly what happens to the mind in meditation. You put your car into the slow lane – the inspirational passage – and you stay there, going through the words of the passage as slowly as you can. Distractions will try to crowd in, and you don't want to leave big gaps for them to rush into. For the most part, though, you just increase your concentration. In this way, little by little, you can gain complete mastery over the thinking process.

ONE-POINTED ATTENTION

I really want to help my community and the world. Why do our efforts seem to have so little effect?

Most of us have minds that are scattered or distracted: sometimes positive, sometimes negative, constantly changing with our shifting moods and desires. Flickering attention is a sure sign of a divided mind. Division is tension. Division is friction. Division is ineffectiveness. Division is futility. And a mind divided cannot stand.

Most of us have a mind that is divided; that is why it some-times cannot stand under the impact of life. It is the concentrated, focused mind that reaches people. All the great changes in the world for good and for ill have come from the impact of men and women with an overriding singleness of purpose and a con-centrated mind. In our own times, on the positive side, Gandhi is a perfect example. To make our full contribution, we need to train the mind to be at peace and then radiate that peace to those around us.

Can you say more about how we can make our full contribution?

Whoever we are, we can improve our contribution to the world simply by giving complete attention to the job at hand in a spirit of detachment. We don't have to compare our lives or work with others'. All that is expected of us is that we give our very best to whatever responsibilities come our way. As our capacity to con-tribute increases, greater responsibilities will come to us. That is the way spiritual growth has always taken place down the centuries.

When I began to meditate, I don't think it ever occurred to me to change jobs or to try to make a "spiritual" contribution with my writing. I simply gave more and more attention to my teaching—to my colleagues and especially to my students. I was meditating every day on the words of the Bhagavad Gita, where Sri Krishna counsels: "Do your best; then leave the results to me."

What does it mean to work in a spirit of detachment? And how does it tie in with one-pointedness?

It is helpful to keep each of these three aspects in mind — attention, detachment, and the job at hand. But before I comment on them, I want to emphasize that they are really not separate. They are three elements of a single skill.

When you dedicate yourself to the task at hand with complete concentration and without any trace of egotistic involvement, you are learning to live completely in the present. You are making yourself whole, undivided, which is the goal of the spiritual life and the meaning of that much-misunderstood word *yoga*.

In reality, all these three amount to unifying our attention. We don't usually think in these terms, but when we ignore responsibilities, we are actually dividing our attention. When we postpone or neglect a task that needs doing, we are dividing attention. When we do a job halfheartedly, we are dividing attention.

Even when we get personally entangled in our activities, we are dividing our attention. And if "dividing attention" sounds abstract, let me assure you it is utterly practical. When we divide our attention, we split ourselves, which weakens everything we do. In this sense, perhaps the simplest expression of our goal in meditation is that we are trying to make ourselves whole.

How do we do this in practice?

Let me offer a few practical suggestions from my own experience.

Over time, every job becomes routine. For a year or two everything seems new; every task presents an interesting challenge. But after a few years, it's "Oh, another patient, another client, another performance, another report." New things have a way of becoming old; new hats become old hat; everything becomes passé.

The answer is not to change jobs, drop out, or walk away, but to give more attention and do the very best we can. With complete attention, everything in life becomes fresh.

Therefore, the Gita says, don't ask, "Is this interesting? Is this exciting?" If a job is exciting today, it's going to be depressing later. Unless it is at the expense of life, give it your very best. Doing a routine job well, with concentration, is the greatest challenge I can imagine. You're not just doing a job but learning a skill: the skill of improving concentration, which pays rich dividends in every aspect of life.

Finally, in attending to the task at hand, the Gita urges us never to get attached to personal pleasure or profit. Whatever the job, do it as a service to others. Don't do it to gain credit or prestige or to win attention.

Sometimes people ask me incredulously, "You mean you're not interested in the results of what you do?" Of course I am interested. I doubt that there is anybody more interested in his work than I am, because I know how much people can benefit from what we are doing at the Blue Mountain Center of Meditation. But after many years of practice, I have learned to do my best and then not worry about whether things will work out my way.

I work hard and I worry a lot. What can I do to stop worrying?

This habit of worrying is a significant comment on our times. I know people who put a great deal of effort into developing this habit. When they leave home, they worry about whether they have locked the door; they have got to go back and turn the key in the lock to make doubly sure. Then they realize they have left the letter inside and worry whether they have remembered to write the address. If we lock the door and mail our letters with attention on what we are doing, these little problems don't arise at all.

It is in these small matters of daily life that lack of concentration shows up easily. People worry because they don't concentrate. Whatever you are doing, give it your full attention. We can guard ourselves against tension by learning to be mindful in everything we do.

Similarly, when the day is done, leave your work at the office. Many people who work hard bring their work home with them, yapping like a poodle at their heels. At the dinner table, when they sit thinking about their deadlines and responsibilities, the poodle is nestled under the chair, whining away. They curl up with it at night and dream about reports that haven't been filed, statistics that don't point to the right conclusions, mail that hasn't been responded to or that has been sent out with the wrong memo attached. This is what I mean by bringing the poodle home: it's not just in your briefcase, but in your cranium too.

It takes a lot of control to work with concentration for eight hours and then drop your work at will, but this is one of the greatest skills that one-pointed attention can bring. When you enter your office, you give all your attention to your job; once you leave, you put the job out of your mind. This simple skill guards against tension and allows you to give your very best. If you have given your best, there is no need to worry about the results.

Could you explain how one-pointedness can help in conflicts?

The person who can give undivided attention when others are being unpleasant is a real peacemaker. Slowly he or she can disarm the hostile person simply by listening without hostility, with complete and loving attention.

When you see opposition, do not get afraid. Look upon tough opposition as a challenge to test your inner growth—to see if your capacities have grown so that through patience, courtesy, and the depth of your conviction, you can win over your opponent into a fast friend.

But all this takes time, and it takes the capacity to concentrate. You have to be willing to develop these skills, which is the purpose of slowing down and one-pointed attention.

How does a one-pointed mind help with our interpersonal problems in general?

Many problems that we take for granted are not really necessary; they arise from attention getting distracted and caught without our consent.

For example, all of us are familiar with the toll negative memories can take. When they come up, they simply won't let us alone. They claim our attention, and dwelling on them only makes them stronger. The mind gets upset until finally the body begins to suffer. But if you can turn attention away, just as you do in meditation, the memory will gradually lose its emotional charge. The memory itself is not lost; it simply loses its compulsive hold on you.

Again, when a friend has offended you, it is not your friend that causes the agitation; it is dwelling on what happened. Attention is caught, and the mind cannot stop thinking about it. When you go to the theater, you can't pay attention to the film. When you go to bed, you can't stop thinking about what happened, so you toss and turn all night. Dwelling on resentment or hostility or any other negative emotion magnifies it; the answer is to turn attention away.

Happiness comes when we forget ourselves, and misery when we can't think about anybody else. This is essentially a problem of attention getting trapped. One of the greatest benefits of meditation is that it releases the precious faculty of redirecting our love and attention from our little selves so it can flow towards other people. It's an exhilarating experience, because most of us have no idea of the capacity for love we have imprisoned.

TRAINING THE SENSES

Could you explain how training the senses helps meditation?

Attacking the mind directly is extremely hard. But there is something we can attack directly to deepen meditation, and that is eating. Through our eating habits — especially likes and dislikes in eating — we can learn to get at the mind indirectly.

You can begin simply by ceasing to choose foods that don't benefit your health and instead choosing foods that do. With this simple resolution, you'll strengthen your will and deepen your meditation — and please your physician, too.

I first became interested in changing my diet for the better under the influence of Mahatma Gandhi, when he was writing weekly articles for his paper *Young India*. Diet was an important topic for him, and he experimented all his life to discover the very best. Indians can be quite traditional about food; they always want the dishes that mother used to make. But Gandhi put tradition aside in favor of health, and his example appealed to me deeply.

I too, of course, had been brought up on Indian cuisine – first Kerala style, later Central Indian. And I had enjoyed it all thoroughly. It never occurred to me to ask what the purpose of food is. Gandhi's example prompted me to ask; and I concluded, to my great surprise, that food is meant to strengthen the body. So I started changing. I began to eat fruits and vegetables that wouldn't have appealed to me in earlier days at all. As I began to focus more on health, I found that I enjoyed salads, and that highly spiced curries no longer seemed palatable. I was prepared now to agree with Gandhi's dictum that taste lies in the mind.

Today, if I were to eat junk food, my body and palate would protest. I work every day from morning till night, every day of the year, and the energy for this kind of work comes partly from food. Eating what gives you energy for selfless service, keeping your body healthy and light, is a matter of teaching your taste buds what to enjoy.

As always, the purpose here is training the mind. With training, your senses begin to listen to you, and when your senses begin to listen to you, your mind becomes calm and clear. Then you always have freedom of choice.

You've talked about the joy of actually defying desires. Could you explain what you mean by that?
I don't think I really understood what Gandhi was getting at until much later, when I began to meditate. It was then that I made

what was for me a remarkable discovery. When I needed a lot of drive to go deeper in meditation — for example, if I had a problem to solve that required more energy and creativity than usual — I found that I had only to pick a strong sensory urge and defy it. When you suddenly need cash, don't you go and shake the piggy bank? It was a little like that. I would look around intently to see what kind of cravings I had, and then I would walk up to a really big one and say, "Come on, because I am really broke." The desire would come on strong, and I would push it back and come out with both my pockets loaded.

My whole outlook on desire changed. Formerly, when a strong urge would come, I used to do what everybody does: yield to it, and not reluctantly either. Now I began to rub my hands with joy at the prospect of doing just the opposite. "Here's another desire! It's strong, so I'll gain even more by defying it." I began to understand that any strong desire, when it is defied, generates a lot of power.

Not every desire, I should say, is to be rejected out of hand. I distinguish very carefully between harmless desires and desires that are harmful to the body or mind — or, of course, to those around you. If the desire is for food that is wholesome, you may well be able to yield with full appreciation. But if it is a desire for something sweet that you don't need, you will find you can get equal satisfaction out of refusing it. It's a deceptively simple change in perspective. Your attitude toward the body becomes very different: you see it no longer as an instrument of pleasure, but as an instrument of loving service.

Isn't it all a bit grim?

You don't have to give up all desires to be strong; you just have to give up all selfish desires. For example, when you have food that strengthens the body, especially when it is cooked and served with love and eaten in the company of family or friends, you don't need to pass it up just because you like the taste of it. The Lord would say, "Dig in; I am in that desire too."

I am very much like my grandmother in this respect. When there was a feast coming I don't think she ever thought about the food before or after; but while she was eating I have never seen anyone enjoy a meal more. At our ashram, whenever there is a special occasion, whether it be Jewish or Christian, Hindu or Muslim, we really have a feast. And when someone comes in and puts a steaming platter of blintzes on the table, we don't turn our eyes away and say, "We can't eat blintzes; they're not mentioned in the scriptures." We sit down, repeat the mantram, and polish them off.

The question in all these matters is, are you doing this for yourself or for others? In other words, we don't need to turn our backs on the innocent delights of life to be spiritual. We can participate fully in life as long as we are trying our best to put those around us first.

Why do you advocate a vegetarian diet?

Vegetarianism not only helps us to maintain our health on the optimum level but also has the spiritual purpose of deepening our awareness of the unity of life.

I am fortunate in being born in a Hindu family that has been vegetarian probably for over a thousand years, but I am not a vegetarian because my ancestors were; I am a vegetarian because I have come to know that I form one unity with everything around me. As our spiritual awareness deepens, we will come to have great compassion for animals and will never want to be a party to their ill-treatment. Vegetarianism affirms the unity of all life.

One of the remarkable developments in meditation is that even if we take to meditation without any desire to practice these related disciplines, after a while we will be drawn to them. The changeover, for example, from nonvegetarian to vegetarian food can be made gradually.

Could you explain the link between training the palate and improving relationships?

That was a personal discovery. I soon found that by loosening compulsive likes and dislikes about food, I was undoing the whole habit of disliking. It paid immediate dividends in personal relationships. I didn't have to dislike someone just because I disagreed with his opinion or because she disliked me. This kind of realization disarms people, and I soon found that all my relationships had improved.

What is the real purpose of juggling likes and dislikes?

Juggling with likes and dislikes is much more than learning to be flexible about the relative merits of foods or jobs or people. The real issue is freedom. Our habitual responses in small matters reflect the way we respond to life itself: the person with rigid tastes in food is likely to have rigid tastes in other fields as well. All of these hold him hostage. He is happy so long as he gets everything the way he likes it. Otherwise — which may be ninety-nine percent of the time — he is unhappy over something. He might as well be bound hand and foot.

My grandmother used to tell me, "Don't ever beg from life." Life has only contempt for people who say, "Please give me two things I like today: one in the morning, preferably just before lunch, and another about midway through the afternoon, when I start to get irritable. Oh, and please remember to keep everything I dislike at a convenient distance." This is panhandling, and we usually get what we deserve: disappointment, with a capital D.

We are not beggars, Granny would say; we are princes and princesses. We can learn to say to life, "It doesn't matter what you bring today. If you bring something pleasant, I will flourish; if you bring something unpleasant, I will still flourish." Once we have tasted the freedom of juggling at will with our personal preferences, we can face whatever comes to us calmly and courageously, knowing we have the flexibility to weather any storm gracefully. This is living in freedom, the ultimate goal of training the mind.

You say we should be careful with our media choices, but my friends think I'm being overly strict. Why's it so important?

You know the slogan "You are what you eat." I would say, "No, your body is what you eat. You are what you think." Just as the body is made of food, the mind is made of thoughts: everything we think, feel, and take in through the five senses.

Of course, there are books and movies and even television shows that provide good entertainment and good education. The point is to be able to choose. With junk food so readily available, most of us have learned to be selective about what we put into our mouths; why not be careful about what we let into our minds?

Nutritionists remind us that before we eat something, we should ask, "Do I want this to be part of my body?" Similarly, we should remind ourselves every time we go out for entertainment or switch on the TV, "This experience is going to become part of me. Will I be the better for it? Will it leave me calmer, or will it agitate me? Will it make me more compassionate, or will it stir up anger or leave me depressed?"

In other words, I am talking about learning to make choices — reclaiming the power to choose what goes into your mind. After all, don't you like to choose the food you eat? It is the same with what you feed your mind.

The spiritual life is hard work at times, and then I really need some relaxation. What sorts of entertainment do you recommend?

Entertainment is essential for all of us. Recreation is part of spiritual living. I look upon everything I do as part of my spiritual practice. So I take great care that what I see and hear is likely to be innocent entertainment – with a good story, good cast, good direction, but none of the degrading drawbacks I have come to expect on the stage or screen.

As a former professor of English literature, I enjoy classics. But nourishing entertainment need not be great art. For years I had tickets to our local college's summer repertory theater, whose plays were selected to please a community crowd. I would take a carload of young friends and stop for ice cream before the show. So leading the spiritual life doesn't mean bleaching the color out of life. We can enjoy all that is wholesome everywhere – in plays, in music, in films, in conversation, in simply being together.

What about vacations? Aren't they important, too?

The mind needs R&R – relaxation and refreshment. But all too often we misinterpret this need, just as we misinterpret a desire for food. We think in terms of escape, "getting away from it all."

And that is what we need – but not in the usual sense. "Getting away from it all" doesn't mean the mind can count on finding refreshment on a beach in the Bahamas. Our real need is to lift the burden of constantly thinking about ourselves.

Someone once asked Mark Twain why he didn't take a vacation. "I would like to," came the reply, "if I didn't have to take that fellow Mark Twain with me." That is the heart of the matter. The best theater in the world would be one that lets us check our ego at the door – and then, I would say, lets us forget to pick it up again when we go home.

This is the secret of healthy entertainment, and understanding how the mind works explains why. The relief we get from a movie or a theater performance doesn't come from the activity. It comes from concentration. When the mind is absorbed in a single focus, it has no attention to give anything else – not even the insistent demands of *I*, *me*, and *mine*.

In this light, any concentrated activity can be right recreation. Sports like tennis that require sustained concentration are particularly good because they exercise the body as well as focus the mind. Even work can be recreation if we get so absorbed in it that we forget ourselves. And to me, the best recreation of all is selfless service – work done for others without any desire for recognition or reward. That is why Gandhi said, "I am always on vacation."

PUTTING OTHERS FIRST

If we put others first, won't they exploit us? I don't want to be a doormat.

Putting others first does not mean saying yes to everyone. Love often expresses itself in saying no. When you allow people to exploit you, you aren't just hurting yourself; you are helping the exploiter to hurt himself as well. To connive at somebody who is not living up to his responsibilities not only doesn't help the situation; it doesn't help that person either.

We aren't helping inconsiderate people when we give in to their demands or let them walk all over us. It only feeds the habit of rudeness to let them have their way. The more insensitive the other person is, the more reason for you to alert your mind to be calm and compassionate and, if necessary, to face opposition firmly but tenderly.

How do we stand up to someone who's making an unreasonable demand — in our family, for instance?

Love often shows itself in the inward toughness that is required to say no to an attitude or desire that we think will bring harm. Parents have to do this often, for children who grow up without hearing no from their parents will be terribly brittle when they have to take no from life itself – and, worse, they will have a hard time saying no to themselves.

But loving opposition, whether to children or to adults you live or work with, has to be done tenderly and without any anger or condescension. Otherwise you are likely only to be adding more self-will to the flames. This is a difficult art. Go slowly, and remember that it is always better not to act in the heat of the moment. Whenever time allows, instead of responding immediately to an unwise demand, take a mantram walk first, meditate, and then speak when you can do so with kindness and patience. Remember, too, that the very best way to change someone is to begin with your own example.

It requires enormous judgment, and bravery too, to oppose nonviolently people we love — to fight the sin but not the sinner. In time, we can lovingly wear them down with our patience, and when we see signs of regret and reconciliation, we make friends again and completely forget the barrier that stood between us.

I get a bit confused about being kind. I know I'm a people-pleaser.

Putting others first is an area in which the mind can often play tricks on us. Interestingly enough, often when we think we are thinking of others, putting their needs first, we are really just trying to please — which means we are really thinking about ourselves. You can see how slippery self-will can be.

I find it very hard not to fight back if someone attacks me. Anything else feels weak.

Strength is often equated with the capacity to attack, but to me it means the internal toughness to take whatever life deals out without losing your humanity. It is those who never stoop to retaliation, never demand an eye for an eye, who are truly strong. They have the toughness to be tender, even sweet, while resisting violence with all their heart. By contrast, those who are ready to strike back at the slightest provocation are not strong but fragile. They may espouse a higher view of human nature, but almost anything can break them and make them lash back at those they oppose.

How did you learn to stay calm and kind under attack?

For those of us who have had our intellects honed, it's very difficult to keep from using sharp words. When you're being criticized or attacked, it's almost considered an intellectual responsibility to answer back with compound interest. And that's just what I used to do in faculty meetings, along with everyone else – until I began to understand that if somebody attacked me, there was no need to get angry. It didn't improve the situation on any level – and besides, something within me rebelled against being bounced around like a rubber ball. So I started repeating my mantram silently and keeping quiet.

This doesn't mean making a doormat of yourself. Just the opposite. It is training – learning to get your mind under control. The first goal is to break the connection between stimulus and response. Later, once you have a measure of detachment, you can reply to criticism without identifying yourself with your opinions or the other person with hers, choosing words that are kind, respectful, and to the point. The key is to have a choice.

Most personal disagreements, I would say, arise from the unwillingness to see the other person's point of view. It is not that we have to accept it, but under no circumstances should we refuse to acknowledge that the other person has a point of view – one that deserves to be listened to with respect and evaluated with detachment.

Most of us acknowledge this in principle, but in practice it is all too rare. It took years of retraining my mind to learn to listen with respect to opinions utterly opposed to mine, weigh them objectively, and either retain my own opinion or revise or throw it out according to what I learned.

When we are able to do this — to be completely loyal to our own ideals while respecting the integrity of those who differ from us — often they begin to respond. What matters is the friendliness we show, the attention with which we listen — and, more than anything else, the complete absence of any sense of superiority. The superiority complex is most rampant where our sense of separateness is inflamed. The less separate we feel from those around us, the less superior we will feel too. Once we grasp this, every disagreement becomes an opportunity for spiritual growth.

Do people always respond positively? What if they don't?

While I was teaching literature, I had a colleague whose manner and opinions were opposed to mine in every conceivable way. I probably worked on that relationship throughout my tenure on campus. Not only did I learn to stay calm when he attacked me; I went out of my way to be kind to him. I don't think the effort ever made much difference to him. Our relationship never changed: I never did succeed in winning him over.

But that didn't matter. What was thrilling to discover was how much I had grown by trying. Because of that challenge, I learned to make myself unshakable in any storm of criticism or ill will. That skill proved invaluable later, and those years of trial gave me one of the most important lessons I have ever learned in personal relationships.

As you learn to be patient, you get confidence. Next time, when a bigger outburst comes, instead of retaliating, being unkind, or making sarcastic remarks, you use the incident to train the muscles of your patience by repeating the mantram.

Have you any emergency advice for when we lose our temper?

Whenever I found myself caught in a foolish situation I used to ask my grandmother, "Granny, if you found yourself in a situation like this, what would you do?" It took years for me to understand her simple answer: "Son, I wouldn't get into a situation like that."

This is very practical advice. Don't get into quarrels in the first place. If you do find yourself getting caught in one, close your mouth, start your mantram, and take the closest exit. If you can, go for a fast walk — even five minutes will help to quiet your mind. You'll be surprised at how effective this is. And when your mind is quiet, you remember the good things the person has done to you and forget the bad things on which you have been dwelling.

Second, throw yourself into highly active selfless work, with a concentrated mind. For a while, your anger may make it difficult to concentrate. If you are very angry, don't deal with powerful machinery. But when you are able to concentrate, your anger will have been transformed into power to help others, to deepen your meditation.

I know I have a tendency to be judgmental. How can I overcome this?

When we keep pointing a finger of judgment at others, we are teaching our mind a lasting habit of condemnation. Sooner or later, that finger of judgment will be aimed point-blank at our-selves. It is not that people do not sometimes warrant judgment; fault is very easy to find. But judgmental attitudes and a sus-picious eye only poison a situation. To right wrongs and help others correct their faults, we have to focus on what is positive and never give in to negative thinking. Love, sympathy, and forbearance require steady strength of mind. Love means that whenever negative thoughts enter the mind, we can turn our attention to positive thoughts instead. This is all that is required to guard ourselves against lapses from love.

The key to this is giving – our time, our talents, our resources, our skills, our lives – to selfless work, some cause greater than our small personal interests. By working hard to give what we can, and by cultivating kindness and compassion under every provocation, we can escape destructive ways of thinking.

This does not mean becoming blind to what others are doing. That is not what mercy and forgiveness mean. I know when some-body is being rude or unkind, but it does not impair my faith in that person or lower him in my eyes. I keep my eyes on the core of goodness I see in him, and act toward him as I would have him act toward me. There is only one way to make others more loving, and that is by loving more ourselves.

But what if the person is really annoying?

The more you learn to change your likes and dislikes at will, the more clearly you will be able to see the core of purity and selfless-ness that is the real Self in everyone. This is seldom easy. Some people are a little more irritating and self-willed than others; there is no doubt about it. But instead of criticizing such people, which only makes their alienation worse, you can focus all your attention on what is best in them.

This is one of the most practical skills I have learned from my grandmother, and it can be tremendously effective in helping those around you. It is something like turning a flashlight on a particular spot. I don't diffuse my attention to take in both positive and negative behavior; I keep concentrating on what is kind, what is generous, what is selfless, and the amazing response is that this kind of support draws out and strengthens these very qualities. Not only that, as they become more secure, such people begin to spread this consideration to their other relationships too.

What about when we're dealing with someone who has treated us badly in the past?

Experience, we believe, does not teach us that others are trustworthy; it teaches us that we had better watch our flanks. The memory of past letdowns can weigh down any sensitive human being, making trust an elusive commodity to acquire. Worst of all, when negative memories cast a shadow of mistrust over our relationships, we lack the vitality we need to withdraw our attention and act with kindness, as if those shadows were not there. That is why any effective reformation of character has to start with reforming the thought process itself.

Here the power of the mantram makes itself felt. Each time your thoughts start to wander down dark alleyways of the past, by drawing on the mantram you can call them back and point their feet in the direction you really want them to go. Gradually, with practice, your thoughts will wander much less frequently;

in time, they may even forget the address of those alleyways they once haunted.

What's at the root of negative tendencies like anger?

All these habits of mind that can make life hell, the mystics say, can be traced to one central flaw of attention. To call it self-preoccupation comes close: the habit of dwelling on my needs, my desires, my plans, my fears. The more deeply ingrained this pattern of thinking is, the mystics say, the more we make ourselves a little island isolated from the rest of life, with all the unhappiness that has to follow. This is not a moral judgment; it is simply the way happiness works. Asking life to make a selfish person happy, my grandmother used to say, is like asking a banana tree to give you mangoes.

But there is a better word for this habit of mind: self-will, the insistent drive to have our own way, to get what we want, whatever it may cost. Self-will has a million forms, but every one of them is a kind of torment. Whenever we feel life is being unfair to us, whenever we hurt because people are not treating us right or paying us attention or giving us our due respect, nine times out of ten what is hurting is our self-will.

Self-will has always been human nature, but today it is almost worshipped in some circles. Unselfishness is considered old-fashioned and unnatural, and to be happy, some professional psychologists say, we have to learn to assert ourselves, attend to our personal needs first, "look out for number one."

To be sure, there are reasons for these extreme positions. People think that being unselfish is boring, that a selfless person cannot possibly enjoy life because he is constantly making himself a doormat, that to have a high sense of worth you have to have a big ego. These are just misunderstandings, but the observation remains true: our age sets a premium on self-will in aggressiveness, competitiveness, and self-aggrandizement; that, we are told, is the route to joy.

I like to think of self-will as love turned around. Love is energy, and self-will is that energy focused on oneself. We can learn to free that energy, and when we do, our lives will fill with love — which is what living in heaven means.

This sounds so difficult. How do we turn self-will around?

Friends often tell me, "But I can't make myself pure! I have very negative thoughts. A person like you wouldn't understand just how negative!" I assure them that indeed I do understand. How many are born pure in heart? Yet in all the major religions, superb teachers have given clear instructions in how to make our minds pure so that divinity can shine forth: how to transform our personality from self-centered to selfless, from unconcerned to caring, eventually even from human to divine.

Intellectual study cannot be of much help in this transformation. Only meditation, the systematic turning inward of attention, can take us deep into consciousness where the obstacles to a pure heart hide.

From this point of view, meditation can be described as nothing more or less than the purification of consciousness, by removing everything that obstructs our vision of the divine core in others and in ourselves.

In meditation, when you go through an inspirational passage such as the Prayer of Saint Francis with complete attention, each significant word or phrase drops like a jewel into the depths of consciousness. With each sentence you are absorbing the loftiest image of human nature. When your absorption in the passage is complete, nothing else will remain in your consciousness. Saint Francis's ideals will gradually displace all negative thoughts, so that little by little, divinity begins to shine through. Your mind is empty of yourself, true; but that is also to say it is full of God.

Invitation to a Journey

NOT LONG AGO, a young forty-foot humpback whale on his way to Alaska became enticed by the lure of San Francisco. He veered off course into the bay, and once inside, instead of deciding he had made a wrong turn and retracing his wake, he chose to push on toward Sacramento. By the time I learned of his plight, he had worked his way into fresh waters and got trapped in the shallows of the Sacramento River Delta — a most uncongenial environment for any salt-water creature, but practically a bathtub for one used to thousands of miles of open sea.

Humphrey, as reporters dubbed him, immediately became a media sensation. Every day, news services carried updates on his predicament around the world, while hundreds of whale-lovers flocked to San Francisco to help the Coast Guard try to rescue him. But Humphrey just kept swimming up blind alleys.

Finally someone hit on the idea of luring him back to the sea by the call of recorded whale songs. Humphrey began leaping joyfully, splashing great sheets of water to the delight of spectators, and churned toward the open ocean at a good thirty miles an hour. Traffic on the Golden Gate Bridge backed up in both directions as fans got out of their cars to crowd at the rails and

cheer. They paid handsome fines, but as one woman told reporters, "It was worth every penny."

Something in all of us cheers when a captive creature breaks
free. We are born for freedom, even if we don't understand what
that means or how to find it. Somehow we sense that we are not
meant to spend our lives in the shallows of pleasure and profit.
We are made for vast spaces, to reach beyond boundaries until,
as an English mystic put it, we are "clothed with the heavens and
crowned with the stars" – born with intimations of a potential
much, much grander than anything we can dream of in the day-
to-day world.

While Humphrey's story was unfolding in the daily news, we
human viewers had the advantage of a higher dimension. We
could look at maps, watch aerial views on TV, and see the scene
whole: the narrow confines of the river delta, the broader bay, the
narrow passage to the sea that Humphrey needed to find. To us
it seemed so simple what to do. But Humphrey had no access
to that higher view. All he could have known was that an interesting diversion had turned into a trap. It's easy to imagine his
panic as he found himself alone and boxed in, with no sense of
where to turn for help from a situation he could not understand.

That is how I felt when I discovered meditation: as if I had been
spending my life cramped indoors and just discovered the real
world. Imagine living in one little room all your life! You would
forget what the outdoors was like. Gradually you would come to
believe there is no such thing; only your room is real. That's why
I identified with Humphrey escaping into the sea. Early every
morning, while the rest of the world slept, I would open the
door of consciousness in meditation, slip inside, and set about

exploring the world within — a world I was making my own.

I like to imagine Humphrey free at last, charging out through the Golden Gate deaf to the cheers of earthbound creatures on the bridge above, into the open sea where he belonged. There's not much to the continental shelf in northern California, and whales swim fast. Within a few minutes he would have been in mile-deep waters again, with half a planet of open ocean to roam in as he pleased.

Then, free to go wherever he chose, he must instead have felt a silent command: "North. Go north. Go home." No details, no map, no companions, no guide, just a direction and a desire in response to an overriding imperative from within: go home.

It is very much like that on the journey of meditation too. Once you turn inward, the words of the passages urge you forward in response to a summons from the very depths of the heart. This need to return to the source of our being is nothing less than an evolutionary imperative — the drive to realize our full human potential. As Meister Eckhart says, "Whether you like it or not, whether you know it or not, secretly Nature seeks and hunts and tries to ferret out the track in which God may be found." Something deep within us must find expression beyond the plane of pleasure and profit; that is our glory as human beings.

Only from a higher level than physical existence can we understand this deep need to find our purpose and our place in life. Because this dimension is as real as the physical — nearer to us even than the body, as the Sufis say — we cannot help living in two worlds, the material and the spiritual. To live fully means being at home in both these realms, and that requires a way to bring the deep wisdom of the heart into daily life.

There are many reasons today why one might choose to meditate — health, concentration, reduced anxiety, deeper relationships, security, serenity, the creative resources for making a lasting contribution with your life. Meditation can help you attain all these goals — or, rather, it provides the path; you will need to do the traveling yourself.

But the path leads much, much farther — as far as you want to go. It opens onto a journey that is literally without end, since its goal is only the beginning of a fully human life. The journey holds challenges enough for the most daring adventurer, wonders and treasures that would make Marco Polo's accounts of Cathay trivial by comparison. It is, without exaggeration, the adventure of a lifetime. I have written this book to be your guide.

Blue Mountain Center of Meditation

The Blue Mountain Center of Meditation publishes
Eknath Easwaran's books, videos, and audio recordings,
and offers retreats and online programs on passage
meditation.

For more information and resources, please visit:

www.bmcm.org

The Blue Mountain Center of Meditation
Box 256, Tomales, California 94971

Telephone: +1 707 878 2369
Toll-free in the US: 800 475 2369
Email: info@bmcm.org

BOOKS BY EKNATH EASWARAN

If you would like more on…

Passages to use in meditation:

GOD MAKES THE RIVERS TO FLOW
An Anthology of the World's Sacred Poetry & Prose
This is Easwaran's personal selection of passages for meditation from the Christian, Buddhist, Hindu, Jewish, Taoist, Sufi, and Native American traditions. Detailed background notes and supporting material are included.

Training the mind:

CONQUEST OF MIND
Take Charge of Your Thoughts & Reshape
Your Life Through Meditation
Feeling trapped by unwanted thoughts and emotions can seem an inevitable part of life. Easwaran draws on teachings from the Buddha to show how we can take charge of our thoughts and function more effectively throughout the day.

Slowing down:

TAKE YOUR TIME
The Wisdom of Slowing Down
When the mind is unhurried, we can be patient, kind, and focused, ready to respond to what really matters in the midst of a busy day. Easwaran offers practical advice and insights on how to slow down.

Choosing and using a mantram:

THE MANTRAM HANDBOOK
A Practical Guide to Choosing Your
Mantram and Calming Your Mind
Easwaran gives comprehensive instructions on how to choose
and use a mantram, and explains how this spiritual discipline
helps us access our deepest resources in the midst of life's
problems.

Daily inspiration:

WORDS TO LIVE BY
Short Readings of Daily Wisdom
With a reading for each day of the year, Easwaran comments on
quotations from the world's great philosophers, poets, saints,
and sages, showing how timeless wisdom can guide us in our
daily lives.

MORE BOOKS BY EASWARAN

STRENGTH IN THE STORM
Transform Stress, Live in Balance and Find Peace of Mind

We can't always control what life sends us, but we can choose how we respond. With stories and practical spiritual techniques, Easwaran shows how to find balance, peace, and wisdom by learning to steady our minds.

ESSENCE OF THE UPANISHADS
A Key to Indian Spirituality

Easwaran comments on the Katha Upanishad, the mythic story of a young hero who ventures into the land of death in search of immortality, and shows how the key ideas of Indian mysticism can help us explore the deeper questions of life.

THE BHAGAVAD GITA FOR DAILY LIVING

Easwaran's magnum opus is a practical verse-by-verse commentary on India's timeless scripture, with stories, insights, and spiritual exercises to help us bring the Gita's teachings into our own lives.
Volume 1: The End of Sorrow
Volume 2: Like a Thousand Suns
Volume 3: To Love Is to Know Me

GANDHI THE MAN
How One Man Changed Himself to Change the World

Easwaran gives a moving account of the turning points and choices in Gandhi's life that made him not just a great political leader but also a timeless icon of nonviolence in the world today.

EKNATH EASWARAN

Eknath Easwaran (1910–1999) was a professor of English literature in India and a well-known writer and speaker when he came to the United States in 1959 on the Fulbright exchange program.

In 1960 he began giving regular classes on passage meditation in the San Francisco Bay Area, including a course at the University of California, Berkeley. In 1961, he founded the Blue Mountain Center of Meditation, which carries on his work today through publications, retreats, and online programs.

Easwaran is the author of thirty-three books on spiritual living and world mysticism, and his Bhagavad Gita, Upanishads, and Dhammapada are the best-selling English translations of these Indian classics in the USA. Over 1.5 million copies of his books are in print.